Sati

HISTORICAL AND
PHENOMENOLOGICAL ESSAYS

Sati

HISTORICAL AND PHENOMENOLOGICAL ESSAYS

ARVIND SHARMA

with

AJIT RAY

ALAKA HEJIB

KATHERINE K. YOUNG

Foreword by

M. N. SRINIVAS

MOTILAL BANARSIDASS

Delhi Varanasi Patna

Bangalore Madras

First Edition : Delhi, 1988

MOTILAL BANARSIDASS
Bungalow Road, Jawahar Nagar, Delhi 110 007
Branches
Chowk, Varanasi 221 001
Ashok Rajpath, Patna 800 004
24 Race Course Road, Bangalore 560 001
120 Royapettah High Road, Mylapore, Madras 600 004

ISBN: 81-208-0464-3

PRINTED IN INDIA
BY JAINENDRA PRAKASH JAIN AT SHRI JAINENDRA PRESS, A-45 NARAINA INDUSTRIAL AREA, PHASE I, NEW DELHI 110 028 AND PUBLISHED BY NARENDRA PRAKASH JAIN FOR MOTILAL BANARSIDASS, DELHI 110 007.

"I got married when I was nine, *Hare Ram, Hare Ram,*" she tells me. "My husband was thirteen, and we were both from orthodox Banya families. I had been brought up hearing that our women ancestors in Rajasthan used to commit suttee and afterward were worshipped as goddesses. As soon as I got married, I thought of committing suttee, so that I, too, would be worshipped, *Hare Ram, Hare Ram.* I didn't know you had to be a widow before you could commit suttee. I found out just in time, *Hare Ram, Hare Ram*".

Veda Mehta, *Mahatma Gandhi and His Apostles*
(London: Andre Deutsch, 1977) p. 58

CONTENTS

FOREWORD ix

PREFACE xv

1 Sati: A Study in Western Reactions 1

2 The Tradition of Indigenous Protest against Sati 15

3 An Analysis of the Reaction of Hindus and Non-Hindus to Sati 19

4 The Role of the Brāhmaṇas in the Commission of Sati 25

5 Brāhmaṇa Widows and Sati 29

6 The Scriptural Sanction for Sati in Hinduism 31

7 The Identification of a New Form of Sati 39

8 Raja Rammohun Roy (1772-1833) and Bal Gangadhar Tilak (1857-1920): A Comparison Based on Roy's Attitude towards Sati 43

9 Widows are not for Burning: Native Response to the Abolition of the Sati Rite 49

10 Widows are not for Burning: Christian Missionary Participation in the Abolition of the Sati Rite 57

11 The Bhagavadgītā: Its Role in the Abolition of Sati 67

12 Sati, Widowhood and Yoga 73

Notes 85

Bibliography 115

Sanskrit Index 121

Author Index 123

Subject Index 126

FOREWORD

This book consists of twelve essays on sati, nine of which are by Dr Arvind Sharma of the Department of Religious Studies at the University of Sydney, two by Dr Ajit Ray of the Australian National University Library, Canberra, and the last by Dr Alaka Hejib and Dr Katherine Young, of the Faculty of Religious Studies at McGill University, Montreal. While both Dr Sharma and Dr Ray examine sati in the context of the Indo-Western and in particular in the colonial and Hindu-Christian encounter, Drs Hejib and Young try to look at the institution as orthodox Hindus saw it. The two approaches are radically different but complementary and welcome.

Dr Ray focusses his attention on the part played by various groups and individuals in the abolition of sati, and he comes to the conclusion that the missionaries have not been given their due for the role they played in its abolition. His verdict, however, is not unequivocal, and its unequivocality highlights, in my opinion, a crucial problem in the evaluation of the missionary contribution to the abolition of sati and other humanitarian tasks. He writes: "The Christian missionary involvement for the abolition of the sati rite was only an offshoot of their grand design in India which was the conversion of the country to Christianity." It is not that they were not moved by compassion for the victims of sati but that the desire to demonstrate the superiority of Christianity to Hinduism was there, as also the feeling that in the conversion of Hindus to Christianity lay the solution to their many social ills. And this was before the abolition of slavery in the Western world, to mention but one home-grown evil.

As already mentioned, Dr Sharma also discusses sati in the context of the Indo-Western encounter, of which the Indo-British encounter is only a part, though a decisive one. He points out that the institution is an old one, though it does not have sanction of the Vedas. Even the *Smritis*, the lawbooks, do not sanction sati unreservedly. There is no mention of sati in Manu. Further, suicide is a sin as also killing a woman. The widow who leads a celibate life and performs the prescribed sacrifices for her dead husband, is living according to the injunctions of the *Smritis*. But in spite of this sati seems to have found acceptance in the later *Smriti* literature, between 9th and 11th centuries A.D., to be specific. How did this occur? This is indeed a problem for historical research.

The abolition of sati did not, however, put an end to its polemical role. According to Dr Sharma, "The polemical position to be set out was that India was a country where horrid rites like sati prevailed. These were stamped out by the British. If the British left India, India would lapse into barbarism again." The British tried to "sensationalize" sati, and according to British historians, it was abolished entirely due to British efforts. According to Edward Thompson, "The credit is almost entirely personal, and it is Bentinck's." Percival Spear did mention Rammohun Roy but added, "Rammohun Roy accepted Jesus as one of the religious masters."

Such "hogging" of credit annoyed—and continues to annoy—many Indians. For it needs to be remembered that the Tantrics denounced sati in strong terms. Akbar and some Maratha chiefs fought against it. Albuquerque abolished it in Goa in 1510 A.D.

The Indian response to the British condemnation of sati was, according to Dr Sharma, to "trivialize" the institution, and to scandalize Western womanhood. Indian scholars, for instance, pointed out that sati was not prevalent in the Vedic period and that there were few references to it in the period 300-700 A.D., and that only after 700 A.D. had it gained ground. Its incidence was really local, and limited to certain classes: "It was thus pointed out that the rite was largely confined to Bengal and Rajputana, and among the Rajputs and the Marathas who claimed Rajput descent. It was thus narrowed down into martial custom (though Brahmins also took it over)."

While the motive behind the efforts to determine the temporal, spatial and other dimensions of sati may have been to minimise its gravity, such determination is obviously essential to its understanding. In the first place, Bengal and Rajasthan were its strongholds, and castewise, the institution seems to have been confined to the high castes, and in particular Kshatriyas and Brahmins.

In view of the fact that the two areas of concentration of sati are in northern India, one is tempted to ask whether it was tied up with the institution of hypergamy, and the incidental phenomenon of polygyny at the top of the hypergamous hierarchy. The late Dr Kane thought that the high incidence of sati in Bengal was related to the Dayabhaga law in which the widow had a right to her husband's property till her death, a fact which gave the husband's agnatic relations an interest in her committing sati.

With regard to the rise in the incidence of sati in Bengal between 1815 and 1817, Marshman noted that it was probably due to the emulation of expensive European habits by natives, and to the jealousy of old men with young wives. What is significant in Marshman's explanation is the effort to explain one social pehnomenon—sudden rise in sati—by reference to other social phenomena. Only thorough research into the conditions obtaining in Bengal in the first two decades of the 19th century will make clear whether there is any substance to Marshman's explanation.

It is necessary to make clear here that all widow-burning is not sati. *Jauhar*, for instance, was the collective suicide of Rajput widows who preferred death rather than submit themselves to being captured alive by Mughal troops victorious in battle. Death was preferred to dishonour, and it was fundamentally different from a situation where a widow climbed the pyre of her dead husband to become a sati.

That brings me to the last and fascinating essay, "Sati, Widowhood and Yoga" by Alaka Hejib and Katherine Young. Their declared aim is to see sati as orthodox Hindus saw it: "There seems to be little scholarly attempt to understand what is *Hindu* about the Hindu widow and the sati. Stripped of this adjective Hindu, the widow is like any other bereaved person and the sati is nothing but a suicidal or homicidal act." They then proceed to explain the logic of sati in terms of the ideas and values of orthodox, high caste Hindus. They explain why the sati, the wife who performed sati, became a sainted figure while the widow, in spite of her celibacy and her austere conditions of living, and her preoccupation with matters religious, was regarded as an inauspicious person whose presence boded no good for those around her. Their interpretation makes it clear that even the foreigners who admired the courage and devotion of satis who climbed the funeral pyres of their dead husbands and calmly allowed themselves to be burnt, did not fully understand the institution. The sati was a model wife, and her voluntary death proclaimed the truly transcendental character of the conjugal relationship. It brought renown to her natal and conjugal lineages and to the region, and more importantly, it augured well for everyone. On the contrary, her turning away at the last minute from the ordeal brought infamy to her kin, and forebode disaster for the locality.

I have, however, a difficulty with the interpretation of Drs Hejib and Young: it is not always clear when the authors are merely giving expression to traditional Hindu ideas and when they are putting their own gloss. The Yoga analogue is indeed impressive in helping to understand the sati's behaviour, but was that really how the indigenes saw it? Some more evidence than is presented in the essay, would appear to be necessary.

There is a still deeper level of explanation of sati which needs to be adumbrated here. Between the end of the Vedic period and 12th century A.D., the idea seemed to have gained ground that the husband should have exclusive and total control over his wife's sexuality. Pre-pubertal marriage was the surest way to make certain of it. Pre-pubertal marriage also transferred the responsibility for safeguarding the girl's sexuality from her male kin in her natal family to her husband and his agnates. Once married, total faithfulness was expected of the wife, and this was attempted to be assured by the deification of the husband. Total control over her sexuality was not only for the duration of the marriage: it extended to the pre- and post-marital periods, absurd as it may seem to outsiders. Virginity in brides was ensured by pre-pubertal, and frequently, child marriages, while celibacy was required of the widow. She was disfigured by having her head shaved, and by forbidding to her the symbols of the happy and auspicious state of *sumangalihood* (i.e., the married state with the husband alive), and her activities were restricted to the kitchen and to ritual. She was condemned to perpetual mourning, as it were, and she became a symbol of inauspiciousness and ill-luck. The death of her husband was attributed to the sins she had committed in a previous incarnation. The widow who decided to commit sati was, on the contrary, the mirror image of the widow who had decided to live. She was auspicous, and she was dressed as a bride for her last journey. Her martyrdom brought good reputation and good luck to her kinsfolk and to her village. In some parts of India, memorial stones were erected to satis.

While the widow and sati were treated so radically differently, the ruling idea in both the cases was the assertion of the dead husband's total control over the wife's sexuality. The wife, on the other hand, had no such exclusive right over the husband's sexuality. Not only was a widower not required to burn himself on his dead wife's funeral pyre, he was urged to marry soon. He emerged from mourning after performing the thirteenth day ceremonies. This one-sidedness is really the key to the relationship.

M.N. Srinivas

Department of Sociology
University of New England
Armidale

PREFACE

I would like to begin by specifying the authors of the various essays. Chapters 1-8 and 11 are by Arvind Sharma of the Department of Religious Studies, the University of Sydney, Australia. Chapters 9-10 are by Ajit Ray of the Australian National University Library, Canberra, Australia and Chapter 12 has been co-authored by Alaka Hejib and Katherine K. Young of the Faculty of Religious Studies, McGill University, Montreal, Canada.

In a work of this kind some overlap, even repetition is inevitable. It may even be desirable, for the themes which recur most—the indigenous tradition of protest against sati, for example—are precisely those which have been consistently overlooked. Again, in a collective work of this kind the style and format used by the different authors, not to say their approach, is also likely to differ. These differences have been preserved, for what brings these pieces together is not that they speak with one voice or in a uniform manner but that they address the same subject.

Most of the essays are historical in nature, dealing, as they do, with the phenomenon of sati and it is hoped that they present fresh material and generate new perspectives; the last paper tries to break new methodological ground in attempting a phenomenology of the phenomenal.

A short terminological note on the word sati itself may be helpful to readers. Although there is a tendency to abandon the word Suttee in favour of sati, sometimes the distinction has been preserved on the ground that Suttee may more appropriately describe the act and sati the person committing it. Similarly, with the word sati itself an effort could have been made to use the form sati (without the diacritic) for the rite and sati (with the diacritic) for the person. After reviewing these uses, however, it was decided to use the form sati to cover all cases.

One more prefatory remark also seems called for. It has already been mentioned that this study relies mainly on history and phenomenology but may also, according to an anonymous referee, be described as "humanistic or from the humanities and to my knowledge, is original. Most interpretations of sati in recent years are sociological, anthropological and socio-economic". Those interested in other perspectives may profit by looking at Mary Daly, *Gyn/Ecology: The Metaethics of Radical Feminism* (Boston: Beacon Press, 1978) Chapter III; Dorothy K. Stein, "Women to Burn: Suttee as a Normative Institution" in *Signs* (1978) 4(2): 253-273; Ashis Nandy, *At the Edge of Psychology* (Delhi: Oxford University Press, 1980) pp. 1-31; etc.

The following news item, which appeared in *The Australian* (September 29, 1986, p. 4) should dispel any lingering doubts about the relevance of the present study.

WIFE'S SACRIFICE

> New Delhi: Hundreds of villagers stood by approvingly as a newly wed Indian woman, unable to bear her husband's death, jumped into his funeral pyre in accordance with the banned ancient Hindu custom of sati, the Press Trust of India reported yesterday.

It is interesting to speculate on how attitudes to sati might change if Hinduism becomes a success-oriented religion instead of remaining a sacrifice-oriented religion. The Kerala tradition, which connects Śaṅkara with a kind of Advaitic triumphalism also credits him with the abolition of sati (P.V. Kane, *History of Dharmaśāstra* Vol. II pt. I, p. 506).

The press in India is still aflame with controversy caused by the sati of Roop Kanwar last year as this book goes to the printers. A recent issue of the monthly *Seminar* (February 1988) is devoted to Sati, while the governmental legislation banning glorification of sati has already resulted in the banning of a film on "The ground that it glorified the cult of *Suttee*" (*The Economist*, 20 February 1988, page 94). It has even entered the arena of political controversy, with the disclosure by Ms. Jayalalitha in a mass-circulated Tamil weekly that she contained her desire to commit Sati" as she stood next to the body of MGR, the late Chief Minister of Tamil Nadu and former actor whose leading lady she had been, as a result of being "subjected to untold misery by her opponents in the party". "Tongues have started wagging over her confession, as the legally wedded wife of MGR is still alive" (*Sunday*, 21-27 February, 1988, page 95). This touch of levity may lighten the burden of our theme but cannot detract from its gravity as highlighted in a recent special issue of *Manushi* (Sep.-Dec. 1987).

Finally, permission to publish articles from the *Journal of Indian History*, *Journal of Karnatak University* (*Social Sciences*), *Glory of India*, *Manthan*, *Indica* and the *Indian Economic and Social History Review* is gratefully acknowledged.

ARVIND SHARMA

1

SATI: A STUDY IN WESTERN REACTIONS

Indian widows gone to bed
In flaming curtains, to the dead[1]

G.T. GARRATT

...but the superstition of the Hindoos ...compels the son to set fire to the pile which is to devour the living mother, who fed him ...the heart broken widow, utters her frantic screams ... her flesh palpitates amidst the flames ...[2]

WILLIAM WARD

I

There prevailed in India a customary rite involving the "concremation of the living wife with the dead husband".[3] To this rite was applied the name of SUTTEE in 1787 for the first time with any measure of exactness.[4] Thus, by this term is meant the rite[5] whereby the widow[6] burnt herself at the funeral pyre of her husband.[7] The form SATĪ is also used as a variant and both the forms mean both the rite of widow immolation and the widow so immolated.[8] When the former sense is to be distinguished from the latter, the widow is described as having committed Satī or become one.[9]

This rite of sati has been an element in Western consciousness about India from the 4th century B.C. to our own day.[10] Indeed, the first historical reference[11] to sati is to be found in Greek sources[12] and one of the latest journalistic allusions to it was made in an American magazine. The author speculated, following the uproar that Jacqueline Kennedy's marriage with Aristotle Onassis caused, that perhaps the American public expected Jackie to commit sati upon her husband's assassination.[13]

Although sati has been an element in the Indo-Western encounter all along, its significance in this encounter has varied from age to age and has been quite uneven. This uneven quality of the role of Suttee in the Indo-Western encounter enables one to divide the long stretch of Indo-Western relationship into three major periods: (1) the pre-1757 period; (2) the 1757-1857 period[14], and (3) the post-1857 period, in the light of the role played by sati.

Out of these it is the 1757-1857 period that stands out so far as sati is concerned. It was during this period that the Indo-Western encounter became largely an Indo-British encounter. It was also during this period that sati was abolished so that in the subsequent period it acquired a somewhat lower profile. It, however, continued to play an interesting polemical role (as will be shown later).

II

What was the reaction of a Westerner when he saw a widow burning on the funeral pyre of her husband?

The Greeks provide us with the first account of this reaction. In 316 B.C. the Hindu general Keteus[15] died in the battle between Antigonos and Eumenes.[16] He had two wives; the older one was enceinte. Both of them were eager to commit sati but the elder one was prevented from doing so on account of her condition, at which,

> The elder wife went away lamenting, with the band about her head rent, and tearing her hair, as if tidings of some great disaster had been brought her; and the other departed, exultant at her victory, to the pyre, crowned with fillets by the women who belonged to her and decked out splendidly as for a wedding. She was escorted by her kinsfolk who chanted a song in praise of her virtue. When she came near to the pyre, she took off her adornments and distributed them to her familiars and friends, leaving a memorial for herself, as it were, to those who had loved her. Her adornments consisted of a multitude of rings on her hands, set with precious gems of diverse colours, about her head golden stars not a few, varie-

> gated with different sorts of stones, and about her neck a multitude of necklaces, each a little larger than the one about it. In conclusion, she said farewell to her familiars and was helped by her brother onto the pyre, and there, to the admiration of the crowd which had gathered together for the spectacle, she ended her life in heroic fashion. Before the pyre was kindled, the whole army in battle array marched round it thrice. She meanwhile lay down beside her husband, and as the fire seized her no sound of weakness escaped her lips. The spectators were moved, some to pity and some to exuberant praise. But some of the Greeks present found fault with such customs as savage and inhumane.[17]

The Greeks also had a "theory to account for the custom".[18] This theory was that the custom was designed to dissuade wives from poisoning their husbands.[19]

Thus, it appears that the Greeks had mixed reactions about sati. It was a mix of admiration for the heroic element and condemnation for the savage element in the rite; and speculation about the origin of the rite. These basic reactions cropped up time and again as Westerners confronted the sati rite.

A couple of centuries later Europe started turning Christian; then Islam arose in Arabia and extended its sway over India. The historical landscape altered considerably, yet there is "an almost unbroken chain of foreign reference to the rite, from Alexander's time to our own day: it includes Strabo, Propertius, St. Jerome, Marco Polo, and travellers from Mahommadan lands as well as Christian."[20]

It is from the 16th century onwards, however, in the wake of European navigational expansion, that we find sati once more impinging on Western consciousness and perhaps conscience. And it is also now that the mix of reactions gathers in a new element. This new element enters the picture with the establishment of a beach-head of European imperial expansion in Goa.

In 1498 Vasco da Gama landed in Calicut[21] and soon the Portuguese gained a foothold on the Western seaboard of India in Goa. "After capturing Goa one of the first acts of Albuquerque was to abolish *sati* (1510)."[22] The reaction of European governors, then, as distinguished from those of writers or travellers, was to abolish sati,[23] not just to laud or criticise it.

Another new element in the European reaction was that of romance, yes romance. Thus, Mandelslo was given a bracelet by one of the Satīs and to Thomas Bowrey another Satī gave some flowers from her hair.[24] None, however, can hold a candle to Job Charnock, the founder of Calcutta.[25] "Everyone has heard of how he rescued from the flames a Brahman widow of transcendent loveliness, lived with her happily for fourteen years, set up a magnificent tomb over her body and sacrificed a cock there every year on the anniversary of her death"[26] till he himself died in 1693.[27]

Apart from these new strands in the pattern of European reaction, the old one of mixed reactions continued. There was less speculation about its origins in the 17th and 18th centuries than later, but the curious mix of admiration[28] and condemnation continued to appear. But even here the reactions acquired richness and variety.

Thus, Thomas Herbert, an Englishman who published his accounts of *Travels in Africa and Asia the Great* in 1638, witnessed a sati at Negapatan on the Coromandel Coast. He gives a touching account thereof and then brings it to a poetic conclusion.[29] The Jesuit missionary, de Nobili, also witnessed such scenes in the 17th century. He was impressed "by the ecstatic devotion with which many of these young widows went to their deaths. The spirit in which they did so he found admirable though he felt it could have been expended in a much better cause".[30] J.B. Tavernier, the 17th century traveller, narrates how a widow of twenty-two at Patna "held her hand in the flame of a torch till it burnt to cinders in order to convince the officer that she was a willing party".[31] But he also comments with a touch of irony,

> ...the idolators do not only burn the bodies of their dead, but the bodies of the living. They scruple to kill a serpent, or a louse, but account it a meritorious thing to burn a living wife with the body of the deceased husband.[32]

Where Tavernier comments with irony, Francis Bernier, the

French physician at the court of Aurangzeb, condemns with indignation. He witnessed a sati while journeying from Ahmedabad to Agra at which "five slaves...were so moved with pity and tenderness towards this mistress" who was committing sati that they burned with her. Bernier, however, was not moved, or rather, was moved to indignation.[33]

One thus notices a religious element entering into the reaction. This is manifest in the account of Rev. Mr. Lord, one of the chaplains of the Honourable Company of Merchants trading to the East Indies, residing at Surat, where he witnessed sati.[34] His reactions are discussed in detail in a later chapter.

Thus, we find new patterns emerging in Western reactions to sati. It is interesting to contrast these with the initial Greek reaction. Those reactions were free of any attempt at abolition of sati and were not related to religion. These new elements in the Western reaction may be related to the fact that the Greeks in the 4th century B.C. were not Christians and their attempt to establish themselves politically in India then had proved abortive.[35] In the 17th century Indo-Western encounter, however, the situation was quite different. European powers had already acquired, or were in the process of acquiring, political control over parts of India.[36] Moreover, Europe was now Christian and evangelically so. These differences in the situation of the West may account for the new elements in the reaction to sati. Besides, it is also possible that the number of involuntary satis might have been on the increase. In theory, sati was always optional,[37] in practice usually voluntary.[38] But involuntary sati was not unknown even in earlier times.[39] Moreover, the fact of the special incidence of sati in Bengal, (where the Dāyabhāga law "permitted even the childless widow to become an heir to her husband"[40] might have led to cases of force or undue influence) seems to lend credence to this view.

III

The end of the 17th century closed an epoch in Indian history. Aurangzeb, the last great Moghul Emperor, died in 1707 A.D.[41] and his death was the signal for the disruption of the Moghul Empire.[42] One of the chief beneficiaries of this disruption were the British.[43] These developments opened up a new chapter in the role of sati as a factor in the Indo-Western encounter, for the establishment of British Raj led to the abolition of sati first in Bengal and then in the rest of the country. A brief review of the events leading up to this would be in order.

The British, along with other European nations, originally ventured into Bengal as traders. In the confusion following the dismemberment of the Moghul Empire they involved themselves in local politics and consolidated their position by defeating the local Nawab at the Battle of Plassey (1757).[44] With the acquisition of the Diwani of Bengal in 1765 from the Moghul Emperor[45] they became administrators, in addition to being traders. As traders they had largely been spectators on the Indian scene, now they became actors. In due course this change of status showed in a change of attitude towards sati. Whereas the earlier attitude had been one of passive reaction, of observation and criticism, it could now be one of active intervention, of prevention and abolition. Moreover, just as the flag had followed trade[46] (reversing for a while the famous dictum that trade follows the flag), the cross followed the flag. We have already noticed earlier how a religious element was entering the Western reaction to sati. Now in October 1792 the Baptist Missionary Society had been organised and William Carey and John Thomas were sent to India as its first agents the following year.[47] And the first quarter of the 19th century was distinguished by the activities of the Serampore trio[48] William Carey, Joshua Marshman and William Ward. These activities became specially marked when the ban on missionary activity in British India was raised in 1813.[49]

By the first quarter of the 19th century, then, several strands in the European reaction to sati seemed to be converging on it. It has already been shown how the political European reaction had been in the direction of forbidding it. It was also shown how the European religious reaction had been in the direction of its condemnation as a heathen practice. It took a while for the two to merge, but the thrust was by now quite clear. It was against the continuation of sati. To this in due course was added the force of enlightened Hindu opinion and thus was generated the strong wind which blew out the pyres of sati.

This is how it happened. First the missionary pressure intensified. Each member of the Serampore trio had witnessed actual cases of sati in which force by either covert or overt means had been applied.[50] They condemned the rite forcefully and requested the Government to ban it.[51] In 1816 a tract, devoted primarily to sati, was published which contained the prefatory remark that though the author (who does not appear to have been a missionary) pinned his hopes for its abolition principally on the Government he was "by no means insensitive to the general and direct influence of the British example and especially of the introduction of the Christian religion to remove these evils".[52]

Between 1815 and 1818 the number of sati doubled, from 378 in 1815 to 839 in 1818 in the Presidency of Bengal.[53] The 1815-1818 records—"truly awful records for any Christian Government"[54]—had a disquieting effect on officials.[55] In 1818 "when the pyres blazed most fiercely", Raja Rammohun Roy launched his journalistic attack on the rite,[56] "which aroused such anger that for a while his life was in danger".[57]

In 1821, Raja Rammohun Roy brought out another tract against sati.[58] In 1821 the Nizamat Adalat opined that sati could be suppressed "by proclamation" at least in those divisions where it was little in practice.[59]

In 1823 the Serampore missionaries published a volume containing essays originally published in their periodical *The Friend of India*.[60] The first three of these essays relate to the Burning of Widows and contain a strong attack on sati. In the same year the Court of Directors urged Lord Amherst to prohibit sati but he did not feel inclined to violate the company's traditional policy of tolerance.[61]

In 1825 the number of satis rose again after an earlier decline.[62] This led to a renewal of protests. In 1827 another work attacking sati was published by a missionary.[63]

In 1818 Lord William Bentinck took over as Governor General and started taking a personal interest in the issue. The Governor General consulted the army, the judiciary and native opinion,[64] showing no "undue haste in his preparation for the overdue reform".

Then, one Sunday morning, on December 5, 1829, Rev. William Carey received a document from the Governor General with a request to translate it. The document was no other than Regulation XVII[65] which declared the burning or burying alive of widows as culpable homicide. As soon as Carey received the request:

> Springing to his feet and throwing off his black coat he cried, "No church for me to-day...If I delay an hour to translate and publish this, many a widow's life may be sacrificed", he said. By evening the task was finished.[66]

But the fight was not yet over. The Orthodox Group petitioned the Privy Council on this interference with traditional religious practices. The ship which carried their representative, Mr Bathie, however, sprang a leak and ran aground. Each party interpreted this as an act of Providence in their favour. *Chandrika*, the organ of the Orthodox, believed that Mr Bathie had been spared for a special purpose, a view he himself shared. *Kaumudi*, the organ of the Reformists, insinuated that the content of the petition had something to do with the sinking of the ship. The petition was rejected in 1832—a rejection in which Raja Rammohun Roy played a key role, enhanced by his personal presence in England where he died the next year.[67]

Thus a hardening of the British reaction to sati, aided and abetted by Hindu reformism, led to the abolition of sati. This held true only of British India. The British Government, however, which was on its way towards becoming the paramount power in India, maintained this hard attitude against sati in its dealings with native states,[68] till finally in 1861 A.D., legal sati ceased over the whole of India.[69]

It is clear, therefore, that in the 1757-1857 period the European reaction to sati was primarily one of condemnation, intervention and abolition. The sentiments of admiration and justification had almost evaporated.[70] There was, also, along with this hardening of political attitude a sharpening of criticism against Hinduism. This combination proved highly combustible as the events of 1857 showed, and the "Mutiny"[71] in turn affected the Western perception of sati, as will be shown soon.

It appears that, at least on the face of it, the Regulation of 1829 "suppressed the practice with entire success and without difficulty".[72] Raja Rammohun Roy, however, had warned Lord William Bentinck against a direct and abrupt abolition of the custom.[73] The close association of the political and religious strands in the Western reaction to sati were capable of being viewed as belonging to a noose which was being tightened around the neck of traditional Hinduism. The peremptory abolition of sati is now regarded by most historians as one of the factors contributing to the "Mutiny". The rebel leaders "made capital of the salutary reform".[74]

These developments altered the complexion of reactions to sati. Whereas earlier the abolition of sati had been a joint humanistic enterprise in which the Government, the missionaries and enlightened native opinion[75] had come together on a common platform, from now on the case of sati was to be argued in terms of Imperialism. Sati, on account of its dramatic nature, became an element in the vindication of British Imperialism.[76]

> A Brahman convert to Christ said to us very earnestly a few years ago: "I used to feel very hot towards the English government over what I feel are our wrongs. But when I came to know God and read the Bible, I understood. I saw God was letting the English make return to us for our long neglect and down-treading of the low castes, and of our oppression of the widow."[77]

And of course the most glaring example of this oppression was sati.

Sati was also used as a moral justification to themselves by the Britishers to impose their rule on India. Initially, in the early days of British Raj in Bengal, the "almost unanimous abhorrence of a religion which sanctioned and indeed sanctified burning women alive"[78] had justified it. Now it was justified by asking such leading questions as: Would sati revive if the British left India?[79] Thus, sati played a prominent role in the polemics justifying British Raj in India. The polemical position to be set out was that India was a country where horrid rites like sati prevailed. These were stamped out by the British. If the British left India, India would lapse into barbarism again. This carries us into the next section.

IV

The first period in which we chose to discuss sati, the period which extended from the 4th century B.C. till 1757 was rich in personal reactions. The second period, the period extending from 1757-1857 was marked by a celerity of events which culminated in the abolition of sati more or less over the whole of India. The third period, the period we are about to bite into, the post-1857 period, is remarkable for the manner in which it illustrates the encounter between two cultures when one is under duress.[80] The historical details which occupied us in the previous section are but the one-eighth of the iceberg that lies submerged in the oceanic encounter[81] between two religions and cultures. We now turn to these deeper aspects.

It has been shown how the occupation of Bengal intensified the British reaction to sati; it will now be shown how the Mutiny altered it by creating a need for justifying the British presence in India which had been so violently questioned. A new element now entered the situation.

Sati was to be used as a moral justification for Indians to submit to British Raj.

It became necessary for British writers to SENSATIONALIZE[82] sati on the one hand and for British historians to MONOPOLIZE the credit for having abolished it on the other. Thus, these new strands now appeared in the Western or rather the British reaction to sati.

The tendency to sensationalize sati was not entirely new. Its dramatic quality lends itself easily to sensationalism. Even earlier its visual impact, by arousing the disgust and abhorrence of Englishmen, had caused them to do injustice to Indian thought.[83] Edward Thompson even remarks that the flames of the sati's funeral pyre may have cast deep shadows on Macaulay's Minute.[84] But these effects, if unfortunate, were unconscious. Sensationalization now was deliberate. In order to emphasize the enormity of Hindu opposition to the abolition of sati we are told that a "petition was sent in to the Privy Council, signed by eighteen thousand people, many of whom represented the best families of Calcutta".[85] The fact seems to be that it was signed by only eight hundred people.[86] The lot of the widow is not enviable in

India but to speculate that this was done deliberately to keep her from poisoning the husband sounds a bit far-fetched. But we are assured that this statement was heard from Hindu lips, "We husbands so often make our wives unhappy that we might fear they would poison us. Therefore, did our wise ancestors make the penalty of widowhood so frightful—in order that the woman may not be tempted".[87]

Not only was sati sensationalized, efforts were made to show that to the British alone was due the credit for having abolished it. Thus Edward Thompson recognises Raja Rammohun Roy's role but concludes: "The credit is almost entirely personal, and it is Bentinck's".[88] This is quoted by Harry H. Field to show that it was "not Hindu humanity but British legislation which ended Suttee".[89] This bid to monopolize[90] the historical credit for abolishing sati was so successful that it has become the standard version current in history-books, especially in the West, sometimes even to this day. Thus, P.E. Roberts makes no mention of Raja Rammohun Roy in the context of prohibition of sati.[91] Percival Spear does mention him but then adds "Ram Mohun Roy accepted Jesus as one of the religious Masters"[92] so that again the credit seems to stay with the West.[93]

The fact appears to be that both Hindu scholastic opinion and Hindu government had taken a stand against sati. But to admit this fact would be to undermine the polemical foundations of the British Raj and hence these facts were slighted.[94]

The attempt to monopolize the credit for abolishing sati, however, created another difficulty. If sati has already been abolished, then what is the justification for British Raj anymore, now that sati had been abolished ! The response to this was to show that the concrete manifestation of sati is no doubt gone, but the subtle psychology which underlay sati remains. Thus, the effort was to PSYCHOLOGIZE the issue. Now that the widows cannot burn themselves they suffer "cold Suttee"[95] under Hinduism. What is more, although sati was "finished as an institution, it was never quite done with; you may decide to treat a plant as a weed, but it crops again...".[96] Hence, as if answering the question, "Suttee is gone, now the British should go too", Edward Thompson says, "Suttee has gone, but its background remains".[97] And so, the echo seems to come, must the British?

Indeed, Edward Thompson's book on sati, published in 1928 is of great interest in this connection.[98] It is now generally recognized that the year 1920 represented a turning point in Indo-British relations[99] when a split between India and Britain became irreversible. Political agitation was on the increase and Edward Thompson's work ends with a lament on "the inability of the vast majority of Indians" "to see anything amiss in Hindu civilization or anything that needs to be done in India except political agitation".[100] Obviously, he felt that attention should really be focused on other issues, of which sati is symptomatic.[101]

An investigation of sati, of the history of the rite "sheds light on the dark passages of Indian and British relations".[102] This, however, is not entirely true. Not all writing on sati was designed to suit overt or covert imperial ends. As a matter of fact we find that an old strand reappeared, that of admiration.[103] Sati was idealized as representing "the wholly admirable sentiment and theory, that the union of man and woman is lifelong and the one permanent thing in the world".[104] Thus says Edwin Arnold:

> It was a splendid courage and a beautiful faith that inspired these Indian wives. "Witness that I die, for my Beloved, by his side", was the farewell of the Sati. It was not very wrong of me, it may be hoped, to lay a flower upon the carved stone which recorded where the Sati had last set her fearless little foot upon this earth of selfish hearts and timid beliefs.[105]

Another old strand showed up, that of interest in the origin of the custom. The Greeks had speculated about the origin of the custom, Western scholars now investigated it. It was pointed out early that the alleged references in the Vedas to the rite were based on textual mutilation.[106] Then the question arose: how did sati come to be associated with Hindu practices? Opinions differed. Vincent Smith had little doubt that the sati rite was brought into India by those who "may be called Scythians in a general way".[107] Moreover, the Rajputs "who practised Suttee on such an awful scale and relinquished it so late and unwillingly" were believed to be Scythian in origin. Another approach was to consider widow-sacrifice as something which had once been universal.[108] Traces of it could be found in Greek, Scandinavian,

Gallic and Thracian myths and rites.[109] Thus sati could be viewed as a rite which "belongs to a barbaric stratum which once overlay the world including India",[110] so that it then became possible to "treat the Hindu widow-burning as a case of survival and revival...in accordance with the general ethnographic view on the subject",[111] as a custom which proved "stronger and even more tenacious than Vedic authority".[112] It is easy to see how these explanations helped Hinduism to adjust to the fact that it had once tolerated, at times even encouraged, a rite such as sati. By providing historical and anthropological explanations of the origin of sati these researches seemed to take Hinduism off the hook, so to say, so far as sati was concerned.

V

Thus, sati has been an interesting if not always an important element in the Indo-Western encounter, and an ingredient in the Western perception of India. It aroused a wide gamut of reactions ranging from admiration to outright condemnation, and abolition. Over the long history of Indo-Western contact the emphasis shifted. In what has been called the first period—from 4th century B.C. to 1757—the Western reaction was a mix of admiration[113] and criticism. In what has been called the second period—the 1757-1857 period—the reactions of condemnation and prohibition manifested themselves with vigour leading to the abolition of sati in 1829. In what has been called the third period—the post-1857 period—two opposite trends appeared. On the one hand an approach of broad-based condemnation was developed which used sati as a justification for the perpetuation of British Raj in India.[114] On the other hand, a streak of admiration also reappeared. In this period scholarly investigation into the origin of sati also made considerable headway.[115]

The first Western sight of sati "stirred pity...and in some excess of eulogy...some of the Greeks...reprobated such rites as barbarous and cruel".[116] And thus it has been ever since.[117]

2

THE TRADITION OF INDIGENOUS PROTEST AGAINST SATI

I

It is often not realized that not only in modern, but even in ancient and medieval India, voices of protest against the custom of sati were raised and registered. It is the purpose of this essay to draw attention to this fact.[118] At least three categories of protestants can be recognised: (1) litterateurs; (2) commentators on Smṛtis and (3) Tāntrikas.

II

The famous Sanskrit author Bāṇa (7th century A.D.) was extremely critical of the custom. "In the Kādambarī Bāṇa expressly refers to the case of Uttarā in justification of the conduct of Mahāśvetā in deciding to survive her lover".[119] Along with Uttarā, Bāṇa also "gives instances of famous women" like Rati, Pṛthā and Duḥśalā who "did not resort to sahagamana".[120] A.S. Altekar remarks that to the poet Bāṇa "belongs the credit of offering the most vehement, determined and rational opposition to this inhuman custom".[121] Bāṇa remarks:

> The custom is a foolish mistake of stupendous magnitude, committed under the reckless impulse of despair and infatuation. It does not help the dead for he goes to heaven or hell according to his deserts. It does not ensure reunion since the wife who has uselessly sacrificed her life goes to the hell reserved for suicides. By living she can still do much good both to herself by pious works and to the departed by offering oblations for his happiness in the other world. By dying she only adds to her misery.[122]

III

Some of the Smṛti commentators are quite forthright in their criticism of the custom. Thus Medhātithi (900 A.D.) while commenting on Manu V.157 "compares this practice to *śyenayāga* which a man performed by way of black magic to kill his enemy. He says that though Aṅgiras allowed 'anumaraṇa' it is suicide and is really forbidden to women. Just as the Veda says 'śyenābhicaran yajet' and yet śyenayāga is not looked upon as a dharma, but rather as adharma (vide Śabara on Jaimini I.1.2), so, though Aṅgiras speaks of it, it is really *adharma*; and that a woman who is in a hurry and extremely anxious to secure heaven quickly for herself and her husband might act according to Aṅgiras, still her action is *aśāstrīya* (not in accordance with the śāstras); besides anvārohaṇa is opposed to the Vedic text 'one should not leave this world before one has finished one's allotted span of life' ".[123]

Then Aparārka (12th century A.D.), commenting on Yājñavalkya I.87 cites several texts "which apparently forbid the self-immolation of brāhmaṇa widows".[124] Though Aparārka himself seems to be inclined in favour of sati,[125] he quotes the views of Virāṭa who "positively prohibits the custom. He points out that the widow can do some good to her husband if she survives and offers him the prescribed oblations at the Śrāddha; if she ascends the funeral pyre she will only be incurring the sin of suicide."[126]

Another commentator of the 12th century, Devaṇabhaṭṭa from the South, maintained "that the Satī custom is only a very inferior variety of Dharma and is not to be recommended at all".[127]

Similarly a work of the 13th century, the Smṛticandrikā, "expressly says that anvārohaṇa, though recommended by the Viṣṇu Dharma Sūtra (25.14) and Aṅgiras, is inferior to brahmacarya (leading a celibate life), since the rewards of anvārohaṇa are inferior to those of brahmacarya".[128]

IV

The Tāntrikas, as is well-known, hold not only women but the female principle itself in high esteem. "Even in sacrifices, they insist, female animals should not be immolated. The *Mahānirvāṇa Tantra* prescribes a whole day's fast to the man who speaks rudely to his wife, and enjoins the education of girls before their marriage. The Muslim author of the *Dabistan* says: "The *Āgama* favours both sexes equally. Men and women equally compose mankind. This sect holds women in great esteem and calls them Śaktis and to ill-treat a Śakti—that is, a woman—is a crime".[129]

It should not come as a surprise, therefore, that the *Śākta Tantras* "put a ban on such practices as *sati*".[130] The Tāntrikas "pointed out that woman was the embodiment of Supreme Goddess, and boldly declared that if a person burnt her with her husband, he would be condemned to eternal hell".[131] The *Mahāparinirvāṇatantra* (X, 79-80) quite explicitly condemns sati.[132]

V

It is clear, therefore, that a fairly persistent tradition of indigenous protest against sati existed in India. It should, then not come as a surprise that sati was banned in the Peshwa's dominions even before it was banned in the British territories in India;[133] or that independently of Rammohun Roy, and Lord William Bentinck, Shree Swaminarayan (1781-1830) was already agitating for its abolition in Gujarat by the beginning of the nineteenth century.[133a]

3

AN ANALYSIS OF THE REACTION OF HINDUS AND NON-HINDUS TO SATI

I

Reactions to the rite of sati, in the most usual form of which the widow burnt herself on the funeral pyre of her dead husband, have given rise to expressions of both admiration as well as condemnation.[134] It is, however, generally believed that the Hindus monopolized, so to say, the reaction of admiration; and the non-Hindus that of condemnation. It is the purpose of this essay to demonstrate that such a perception of the situation is erroneous; that there exists a tradition of admiration for the rite on the part of non-Hindus and of condemnation of the rite on the part of the Hindus.

II

The major non-Hindu communities which reacted to this rite are the Greeks, the Muslims and the Europeans, each representing a "clash" between the "indigenous Indian civilization" and "the Hellenistic, the Islamic and the European-Christian" cultures.[135] One finds evidence of admiration for sati in all of these three cultures.

The Greeks provide us with the first historical account of the rite. This account was reproduced in the first chapter. It ends with the comment: "The spectators were moved, some to pity and some to exuberant praise. But some of the Greeks present found fault with such customs as savage and inhumane".[136]

Although it is not clear as to how many of the "spectators" who were moved to "exuberant praise" were Greeks, it is likely that many were, as this instance of sati did not occur within a Hindu but rather a Hellenistic setting. Thus in the very first historical account of sati traces of admiration for the custom on the part of non-Hindus are discernible.

This pattern of admiration on the part of non-Hindus continued to manifest itself in later times. Sati did not even leave some Muslim observers unimpressed, as is clear from the "poem of Muhammad Riza Nau'i, written in the reign of Akbar upon the 'suttee' of a Hindu girl whose betrothed was killed on the very day of the marriage".[137]

> The Hindu bride refused to be comforted and wished to be burnt on the pyre with her dead betrothed. When Akbar was informed of this, he called the girl before him and offered wealth and protection, but she rejected all his persuasion as well as the counsel of the Brahmans, and would neither speak nor hear of anything but the Fire.
>
> Akbar was forced, though reluctantly, to give his consent to the sacrifice, but sent with her his son Prince Daniyal who continued to dissuade her. Even from amidst the flames, she replied to his remonstrances, 'Do not annoy, do not annoy, do not annoy'. 'Ah', exclaims the poet:
>
> *Let those whose hearts are ablaze with the Fire of Love learn courage from this pure maiden !*[138]
>
> *Teach me, O God, the Way of Love, and enflame my heart with this maiden's Fire.*
>
> Thus he prays for himself; and for her:
>
> *Do Thou, O God, exalt the head of that rare hidden virgin, whose purity exceeded that of the Houris, Do Thou endear her to the first kissing of her King, and graciously accept her sacrifice.*[139]

And though the British are associated with the abolition of sati (in 1829), the sentiment of admiration did not vanish even after its abolition. Edwin Arnold's remarks in this connection have been cited earlier.[140]

That sati did not lack British admirers in the 20th century is clear from the observations made by Edward Thompson in his book on sati.[141] He remarks therein that his desire to write his book "dates back to my shame and anger in India when men and women of my own race extolled Suttee".[142]

As with the Greeks, however, expressions of admiration were

matched, perhaps one should say more than matched, by expressions of condemnation of the rite. This is implied in the efforts by the Muslims to abolish[143] the rite and in its actual abolition by the British.[144]

The truth of the matter is that sati aroused mixed feelings in several non-Hindu observers. For instance, the early British travellers of India regularly report instances of sati.[145] William Hawkins (1608-1613) describes sati rather euphemistically by saying that Hindu women "content themselves to live no longer than their husbands",[146] but Nicholas Withington (1612-1616) describes the rite thus:

> Firste shee bewayleth her Husband's Death, and rejoycinge that shee is nowe reddye to goe and live with him agayne, and then imbraceth her Friends, and sitteth downe on the Toppe of the Pile of Wood, and drye stickes, rockinge here Husband's Head in her lappe; and soe willeth them to sett Fyer on the Wood; which being done, her Friends throwe oyle, and divers other Things, with sweete Perfumes, upon her; and she indures the Fyer with such Patience, *that it is to be admired*, being loose, not bounde.[147]

Later British observers, however, show a greater inclination to condemn, probably because by the eighteenth century the rite was being practised indiscriminately and also probably involuntarily.[148] Even Amir Khusrau had conceded that sati and *jauhar* were "no doubt magical and superstitious, nevertheless they are heroic."[149]

III

Among the Hindus, certainly, reactions to sati are characterized by sentiments of admiration. The very acceptance of the custom for centuries and the building of memorials for wives who committed sati testifies to this fact.[150] That even in the 20th century sati had its Hindu admirers is testified to by the frank assertion: "So far from being ashamed of our 'suttees' we take a pride in them; that is even true of the most 'progressive' among us".[151]

It is, however, not often realized that within the Hindu

tradition itself the rite has not been without its critics. The rite became a significant feature of Hindu social life "a few centuries before Christ".[152] What is somewhat puzzling is that "None of the *dharmasūtras* except Viṣṇu contain any reference to *satī. The Manusmṛti is entirely silent about it.*"[153] This seems to *suggest* some kind of a disapproval of the rite but 'argument by silence' can hardly be convincing, certainly not conclusive. It is, however, in some of the commentaries and on Smṛti works that one notices explicit criticism of the rite. The views of Medhātithi (9th century A.D.)[154] have already been referred to in this connection and those of Aparārka (12th century A.D.)[155] as well.[156] Similarly, the negative attitude of Virāṭa,[157] and Devaṇabhaṭṭa[158] towards the rite has already been alluded to earlier. Outside the Smṛti tradition, a well-known passage of Bāṇa (7th century A.D.) which mentions the names of women who did *not* commit sati with approval has also been indicated earlier.[159] Bāṇa also says:

> This, that is known as following one in death is exceedingly useless. It is a way traversed by the illiterate, it is a pastime of infatuation, it is a path of ignorance, it is an act of rashness, it is taking a narrow view of the matter, it is a piece of great carelessness and it is a blunder due to folly that life is resigned when one's father, brother, friend or husband is dead. If life does not leave one of itself, it should not be resigned. If this matter be thought over (it will be seen that) this giving up one's life is for one's own interest; for it serves as a remedy for the unbearable agonies of sorrow, suffered by one's self. It brings no good whatever to the dead man.[160]

The Tāntrika objections to sati have already been cited[161] and the views of Rammohun Roy, who had Śākta links through his mother, are too well-known to require documentation.[162]

IV

For the sake of completion one may now refer to the views of the Muslims in more detail. The ambivalent attitude shown by the Britishers and the Hindus was also shared by the Muslims. As with the Britishers, the Muslims were not as enthusiastic about it as the Hindus, but that they too could sometimes yield to admiration has been pointed out, although the prevailing attitude was one of reprobation. Sushil Chaudhury notes, for instance,[165] that the rite was so patent it was considered a normal feature of social life in medieval India and Muslim sources "fight shy of giving important details about the rite besides occasional references or admiration for it".[163a] The evidence collected by him on Muslim attitudes to sati confirms the ambivalent attitude of the Muslims towards it, but inasmuch as the element of admiration in it has often been overlooked, his conclusion is worth citing:

> It was difficult for Muslims to remain 'without being influenced for long by the custom or the attitude which fostered it'. But it should be noted that cases of direct influence are too few to emphasise the point. However it can be asserted that the influence of sati was limited to those who had an aristocratic Hindu descent or had a predominantly Hindu environment. Jahangir found the rite prevalent among the Muslims of Rajaur who were originally Hindus and converted into Islam by Sultan Firoz. Ibn Batuta tells us that on the rumour of Ain-ul-mulk's death, a rebel against Muhammed bin Tughluq, his wife expressed her desire to be burnt like a Hindu widow. Both Hindus and Muslims went in large numbers to witness a 'Sati' and it can be safely asserted that sati was almost universally admired by people in mediaeval India.[163b]

V

It is clear, therefore, that the reactions of admiration and condemnation towards sati do not divide along cultural lines; in fact, they cross cultural lines. There have been admirers of sati among the Greeks, the Muslims and the British; there have been critics of sati among the Hindus, perhaps down the ages, and certainly from the seventh century onwards. The difference in the texture of the reactions between those of admiration and condemnation is not culturebound. The reaction is not culturally conditioned, though it may be coloured by it; it arises in the heart of human beings in whom acts of ideological martyrdom sometimes evoke admiration and sometimes repulsion. Religious humanism or religious enthusiasm is not the exclusive attribute of any culture but is characteristic of humanity.

4

THE ROLE OF THE BRĀHMAṆAS IN THE COMMISSION OF SATĪ

I

The purpose of this essay is to draw attention to a fact, which, to the best of our knowledge, has hitherto gone unnoticed. The fact is that the role of the Brāhmaṇas in relation to sati seems to have varied from one of *dissuading* the widow from acting onh er resolve to commit sati, to that of *persuading* and sometimes even forcing her to do so. And this shift in attitude has special significance for the nineteenth century.

II

In most of the accounts of sati of the pre-seventeenth century period, in which the role of the Brāhmaṇas can be identified, they appear in the role of persons dissuading the widow from committing sati. Thus "in the early Tamil lyrics we read of an earthly bride *whom the Brahmans seek to dissuade from the sacrifice*; but she answers that since her lord is dead, the cool waters of the lotus pool and the flames of the funeral pyre are alike to her".[164] Similarly, we read earlier of a young widow's resolve to commit sati in the time of Akbar from a poem by Muhammad Riza Nau'i.[165] "The Hindu bride refused to be comforted and wished to be burnt on the pyre of her dead betrothed. When Akbar was informed of this, he called the girl before him and offered wealth and protection, but she *rejected all this persuasion as well as the counsel of the Brahmans*, and would neither speak nor hear of anything but the Fire".[166]

From this point of view an episode in the Mahābhārata is of particular interest. It relates to the death of Pāṇḍu and the subsequent resolve by one of his wives, Mādrī, to commit sati. The critical text of the Mahābhārata at this point only records a quick conversation between Kuntī and Mādrī and then reports that, "Having spoken, the daughter of the king of the Madras, Pāṇḍu's glorious wife by the Law, hastened after the bull among men on his funeral pyre".[167] The Southern Recension of the Mahābhārata,[168] however, represents the sages and the "best of the Brāhmaṇas" as trying to dissuade both Kuntī and Mādrī from their resolve to commit sati.

It is clear, therefore, that on the basis of such literary evidence[169] as we possess the role of the Brāhmaṇas consisted of trying to dissuade the widow from her resolve to commit sati.

III

By, or perhaps in and certainly after, the seventeenth century, however, the situation seems to be changing or to have changed for the worse, if one may inject a value judgement into the discussion. This is revealed by the account of "Rev. Mr Lord, of the chaplains of the Honourable Company of Merchants trading to the East Indies, residing at Surat",[170] of the year 1731 A.D.

In this account, at first the Brāhmaṇas are shown as playing the role of the honest broker, so to say, for "the *brahmins,* as before observed", remarks Rev. Mr Lord, "leave a woman, whom her husband asks in his expiring moments, whether she is willing to follow him in death at her liberty to answer either *yes* or *no. They themselves confess, that the forcing of a woman to it, either by violence or threats, is a crime that merits hell*".[171] Rev. Mr Lord also observes later that while the "seltreas",[172] and *soudras* mix something with the betel which has the property of benumbing the senses, this is not the case with the Brāhmaṇas, for "the *brahmins* say, they never do this, because they would have this sacrifice a voluntary one".[173]

However, Rev. Mr Lord concludes the account by pointing out that when it comes to the actual rite "the woman goes into this hut, sits down on the funeral pile, takes her husband's head into her lap, and puts fire to it with a torch which she holds in her hand, while a great number of *brahmins,* with pokers in their hands, stir up the fire, which they also light on the outward part, *and even push the woman forward, in case the dread of the fires should make her attempt to leap out of it*; but this does not in any way *corres-*

pond with the liberty which they pretend to indulge the woman in on this occasion".[174]

Tavernier, the European traveller in later Mughal times, is already referring to such practices in the seventeenth century. He observes that the Brāhmaṇas that accompany the widow "exhort her to give public testimonies to her constancy and courage: and many of our Europeans are of opinion,[175] that to take away the fears of death, which naturally terrify humanity, the priests do give her a certain beverage to stupefy and disorder the senses, which takes from her all apprehension of her preparations for death. 'This for the brahmins' interest that the poor miserable creatures should continue in their resolutions; for all their bracelets, as well about their legs as their arms; the pendants in their ears, their rings, sometimes of gold sometimes of silver (for the poor wear only copper and tin) all these belong to the brahmins, who rake for them among the ashes, when the party is burned".[176]

Bernier's account, who also travelled through the Mughal Empire at its high noon, confirms that of Tavernier; indeed the "amicable Bernier, indignant at this horrid spectacle, indignantly exclaims against a religion which could permit such a sacrifice; but still more so against '*les demons de brahmens*' who not only encouraged these deluded females, but were the most active persons throughout the infernal tragedy".[177] The later accounts of sati, especially as observed in Bengal, confirm the active role of the Brāhmaṇas in the perpetration of sati.[178]

IV

It had been noted earlier as to how, during the reign of Akbar, who died in 1605,[179] the tradition of Brahmanical dissuasion from the commission of sati was still alive. However, by the time of Bernier's peregrinations in the Moghul Empire from 1656-1668[180] the role of the Brāhmaṇas had reversed from that of dissuasion from sati to the perpetration thereof. Obviously the change could not have been as abrupt as is suggested by the rather uneven nature of such references as are available to us through the accident of survival. Nevertheless, it is clear that somewhere in the transition from pre-Akbar to post-Akbar India the role of the

Brāhmaṇas in the rite of sati underwent a reversal. This paper was intended to draw attention to this fact. Inasmuch as sati seems to have been more prevalent in the nineteenth century A.D. than in any other on the basis of existing records, the question needs to be asked: what was specific to that century which accounts for this increased prevalence and the increased connivance, if not abetment, it implies on the part of the Brāhmaṇas?[181]

5

BRĀHMAṆA WIDOWS AND SATI

I

The purpose of this essay is to demonstrate that (1) sati among the *brāhmaṇas* was originally forbidden and (2) when it was allowed it led to a curious twist in the rules of concremation for *brāhmaṇa* widows because of the exegetical effort to overcome the original ban.

II

It is widely held that the custom of sati was originally either confined to or mainly prevalent among the *kṣatriyas*.[182] More specifically, it was not followed by the *brāhmaṇas*. This situation is best exemplified by the *Padmapurāṇa* (Sṛṣṭikhāṇḍa 49, 72-73) which "extols the custom to the sky, but expressly prohibits it to Brāhmaṇa women. It declares that any person, who will be guilty of helping a Brāhmaṇa widow to the funeral pyre, will be guilty of the dreadful and unatonable sin of the murder of a Brāhmaṇa".[183]

This view also found formal expression in the *smṛti* literature. Thus Hārīta "is positively against the practice being resorted to by Brahman ladies. In his opinion, they, burning themselves, obstruct even the souls of their husbands, from entering into heaven".[184] Similarly, "Several texts cited by Aparārka from Paṭhīnasi, Aṅgiras, Vyāghrapād apparently forbid self-immolation of brāhmaṇa widows".[185]

III

But although "the burning of brāhmaṇa widows began much later than that of kṣatriya widows",[186] begin it did.[187] Now the question arose: how is this to be reconciled with the Smṛti rules forbidding sati in the case of *brāhmaṇa* women?

Two approaches seem to have been adopted to reconcile theory and practice.

(1) Aparārka (12th century A.D.) in his comment of Yājña-valkya I.87 argued that "when death by mounting the funeral pyre of the husband was apparently prohibited to a Brāhmaṇa widow, what was meant was that she should not take the step merely under a temporary sense of overwhelming grief".[188]

(2) Mādhava (14th century A.D.) in his comment of Parāśara IV.31 argued that the "intention may be to interdict death by mounting a separate funeral pyre; a Brāhmaṇa widow must always be burnt along with her husband's remains on the same pyre."[189]

It is the latter "reconciliation" which gained general acceptance. Thus the authors of digests explained away the passages forbidding the self-immolation of a Brāhmaṇa widow "by saying that they only prohibit self-immolation by a brāhmaṇa widow on a funeral pyre different from that of her husband i.e. a brāhmaṇa widow can burn herself only on the funeral pyre of her husband; if his body is cremated elsewhere in a foreign land, his widow cannot, on hearing of his death, burn herself later. They rely on the text of Uśanas that a brāhmaṇa widow should not follow her husband on a separate funeral pyre."[190]

Thus the attempt to reconcile the actual practice of sati by *brāhmaṇa* widows with the *smṛti* injunctions against the practice produced this curious exegetical result. It is interesting in this context that in the *Mṛcchakaṭika*, the objection raised regarding the wife of Cārudatta, a brāhmaṇa lady "was not against Satī as such but to burning in a pyre separate from her husband's".

6

THE SCRIPTURAL SANCTION FOR SATI IN HINDUISM

I

When the practice of sati came under attack at the hands of Christian missionaries and Hindu reformers in the early decades of the nineteenth century, efforts were made to defend it on scriptural grounds.[191] This essay examines the scriptural evidence that could be adduced in defence of sati.

As is well-known, the Hindu scriptural corpus comprises two bodies of literature, *śruti* or revelation and *smṛti* or tradition.[192] It may be noted that in the event of a conflict between the two, *śruti* prevails.

II

What is the evidence from Smṛti literature in support of sati?

(1) The *Viṣṇudharmasūtra* (25.14) mentions sati.[193]

(2) According to Aṅgiras, quoted by Aparārka, "for all women there is no other duty except falling into the funeral pyre, when the husband dies".[194]

(3) There are some verses drawn upon in common, which are found in *Parāśara* IV.32.33[195] and *Brahmapurāṇa* (*Gautamī-māhātmya*) Chapt. 10.76 and 74; and quoted in the *Mitākṣarā* commentary on *Yājñavalkya* I.86 and by Aparārka and also in the *Śuddhitattva*. In these verses:

> Śaṅkha and Aṅgiras say 'she who follows her husband in death dwells in heaven for as many years as there are hair on the human body, viz. 3-1/2 crores of years. Just as a snake-catcher draws out a snake from a hole by force, so such a woman draws her husband from (wherever he may be) and

enjoys bliss together with him. In heaven she being solely devoted to her husband and praised by bevies of heavenly damsels sports with her husband for as long as fourteen Indras rule. Even if the husband be guilty of the murder of a brāhmaṇa or of a friend or be guilty of ingratitude, the wife who dies (in fire) clasping his body, purifies him (of the sin). That woman, who ascends (the funeral pyre) when the husband dies, is equal to Arundhatī in her character and is praised in heaven. As long as a woman does not burn herself in fire on the death of her husband she is never free from being born as a woman (in successive births).[196]

(4) *Śukra* (IV-4-28, 29) "leaves it to the choice of the widow herself, whether to follow her dead husband or to keep living in the world. In the latter case she was incessantly to worship gods, revere the memory of her husband and perform other regular penances".[197]

(5) *Hārīta* says "that woman who follows her husband in death purifies three families, viz. of her mother, of her father and of her husband".[198]

(6) The *Smṛtimuktāphala* and *Madanapārijāta* cite verses, also quoted in the *Mitākṣarā*, to the effect that the "duty of anvārohaṇa is common to the women of all castes from the brāhmaṇa to the caṇḍāla, provided they are not pregnant or they have no young children (at the husband's death)".[199]

(7) Certain verses in the *Bṛhan-Nāradīya Purāṇa* Purāṇa and *Bṛhaspati* provide for the *anumaraṇa*, as opposed to *anvārohaṇa* of *brāhmaṇa* widows.[200]

(8) *Āpastamba* prescribes "the Prājāpatya penance for a woman who having first resolved to burn herself on the funeral pyre turns back from it at the last moment."[201]

(9) *Veda-Vyāsa-smṛti* (II.53) says that "a brāhmaṇa wife should enter fire, clasping the dead body of her husband; if she lives (after her husband) she should give up adorning her hair and emaciate her body by austerities".[202]

(10) The *Bhāgavata Purāṇa* cites an instance of sati and the *Brahmapurāṇa* argues for it. The *Viṣṇupurāṇa* says that the eight queens of Kṛṣṇa entered fire on his death.[203]

(11) The evidence of the epics in regard to sati is of a mixed

nature as will be clear from the following assessment of the evidence:

> The *Mahābhārata*, though it is profuse in the descriptions of sanguinary fights, is very sparing in its references to widow burning. Mādrī, the favourite wife of Pāṇḍu, burnt herself with her husband's body. In the Virāṭa-parva Sairandhrī is ordered to be burnt with Kīcaka, just as in ancient times it is said there was a custom to bury a slave or slaves along with the deceased ruler. The Mausala parva (7.18) says that the four wives of Vasudeva, viz. Devakī, Bhadrā, Rohiṇī and Madirā burnt themselves with him and (chap. 7.73-74) that Rukmiṇī, Gāndhārī, Saibyā, Haimavatī, Jāmbavatī among the consorts of Kṛṣṇa burnt themselves along with his body and other queens like Satyabhāmā went to a forest for *tapas*... The Śāntiparva (chap. 148) describes how a kapotī (female pigeon) entered fire on the death of her husband the bird. In the Strīparva (chap. 26) the Great Epic describes the death ceremonies performed for the fallen Kauravas, but no mention is made of any widow immolating herself on the funeral pyre though the chariots, clothes and weapons of the warriors are said to have been consigned to fire......In the *Rāmāyaṇa* (Uttarakāṇḍa 17.15) there is a reference to the self-immolation of a brāhmaṇa woman (the wife of a *brahmarṣi* and mother of Vedavatī, who when molested by Rāvaṇa burnt herself in fire). The *Mahābhārata* (Strīparva 23.34ff.) on the other hand describes how Kṛpī, the wife of Droṇa, the brāhmaṇa commander-in-chief of the Kauravas, appeared with dishevelled hair on the battle-field on the death of her husband, but does not say that she burnt herself.[204]

Two strands can be detected running through Smṛti literature on the question of sati. Some works either whole-heartedly or half-heartedly advocate it, others do not. As noted earlier, "The *Manusmṛti* is entirely silent about it".[205] A similar division of opinion can be seen among the commentators on Smṛti literature-especially on the dharmaśāstras. Thus Medhātithi argues against sati and Vijñāneśvara for it.[206]

III

One may next ask: what is the evidence from *śruti* literature in support of sati?

Three Vedic passages have figured in the context of the alleged Vedic sanction of sati.

(1) *Ṛg Veda* X.18. 7-8.

According to Aparārka, it is these verses "which render self-immolation free from the sin of suicide"[207] and are thus to be associated with sati, but as P.V. Kane points out:

> The two verses...are employed by the Baudhāyana-*Pitṛmedha-sūtra* in the funeral rites, the first to be repeated when the wife is made to sit near the corpse and the next for making her rise. It is to be noted that Baud. directs that the corpse is placed on the funeral pile after the wife is made to rise from the vicinity of the corpse; while the *Bṛhad-devatā* appears to suggest that the wife ascends the funeral pile after the corpse is placed thereon and then the younger brother forbids her with the verse 'udīrṣva and c.'. But the *Bṛhad-devatā* does not mean that the wife burns herself on the funeral pyre and the brother-in-law contents himself with only repeating a verse to dissuade her. The *Ṛgvidhāna* (III.8.4) says that the brother-in-law should call back the wife of his sonless brother when she is about to ascend the funeral pyre for procreating a son on her with *Ṛg*. X.18.8. It appears that the verse *Ṛg* X.18.8 symbolically describes what even in the days of the *Ṛgveda* was probably only a tradition viz. that in hoary antiquity a wife burnt herself with her husband. In the times of the *Ṛgveda* this practice had altogether ceased, but a symbolical imitation of it had come into vogue, viz. that the wife lay near the corpse in the cemetery and then she was asked to get up and was told that by following her husband to the very doors of death she had fulfilled all that was expected of her and that she should return. The same idea is referred to by the verse 'iyaṁ nārī', but the latter half appears to refer to the practice of niyoga when it calls upon the departed to bestow on the wife offspring and wealth. It is possible to argue that *Ṛg*. X. 18.8 also impliedly has niyoga in view. But both these verses do not expressly refer to the practice of *sati* at all.[208]

Not only Aparārka, the medieval scholiast, but Max Müller, the modern scholar, also sees a connection between *Ṛg Veda* X.18. and the practice of sati, though for different reasons. The verse[209] translates as follows:

> 'Let these women, who are not widows and who have good husbands, sit down with clarified butter used as collyrium; may the wives who are tearless, free from disease and wearing fine jewels (or clothes) occupy the seat in front (first)'[210]

Charles Rockwell Lanman remarks thus on the role this stanza has played in the controversy over sati.

> From Müller's *Essay on Comparative Mythology, Chips,* ii. 34f, or *Selected Essays,* vol. i (ed. of 1881), p. 333f, it would appear that the seventh stanza of our hymn had played a great role in Hindu history. At any rate, this idea is current, and seems traceable to the *Essay.* Here it is stated that the stanza was purposely falsified by an unscrupulous priesthood, *and that a garbled version of it, reading agneḥ for agre, was directly responsible for the sacrifice of thousands of innocent lives.* That the author is in error on these points is argued with great detail by Fitzedward Hall, JRAS. NS. iii. 183-192. He shows that a misreading can be traced to Raghunandana, ca. 1500 A.D., and no further; and that Suttee was deemed to be amply justified by warrants other than those of the Vedic saṁhitā, which was by no means the ultimate appeal for the medieval Hindu.[211]

(2) *Ṛg Veda* X.18.8-9

A.A. Macdonell remarks, on the question of the disposal of the dead, that

> The dead man was provided with ornaments and clothing for use in the next life, the object of the custom being still understood in the Veda (*AV.* 18.4.31). Traces even survive (*Rv.* 10.188.9) which indicate that his widows and his weapons were once burnt with the body of the husband.[212]

Elsewhere he seems to refer to *Ṛg Veda* X.18. 8-9 and *Atharva-Veda* XVIII.3.1 when he says:

In conformity with a custom of remotest antiquity still surviving in India, the dead man was provided with ornaments and clothing for use in the future life. The fact that in the funeral obsequies of the *Rigveda* the widow lies down beside the body of her deceased husband and his bow is removed from the dead man's hand, shows that both were in earlier times burnt with his body to accompany him to the next world, and a verse of the *Atharva-veda* calls the dying of the widow with her husband an old custom. The evidence of anthropology shows that this was a very primitive practice widely prevailing at the funerals of military chiefs, and it can be proved to go back to the Indo-European age.[213]

But as Bhagwat Saran Upadhyaya remarks, after citing these passages from A.A. Macdonell which contain references to *Ṛg Veda* X.18.8 and *Atharva Veda* XVIII.3.1:

These remarks are based on a verse of the *Ṛgveda* which reads as follows: "Rise, come unto the world of life, O woman; come, he is lifeless by whose side thou liest." But this part of the verse is soon followed up by the next line which gives the widow immediately away in marriage to the man who wooes her. It reads: "Wifehood with this thy husband was thy portion, who took thy hand and wooed thee as a lover." The allusion to the lying down of the widow by the side of the remains of her husband's body contained in the earlier part of the verse may be taken to be referring to a feature of the earlier times when widows may have been burnt along with the dead body of their husbands. There is actually a verse contained in the *Atharva Veda* which preserves such a custom of burning the widow and which it calls an ancient religious duty (*dharmam purāṇam*). It is probable that the ancient custom against which the *Atharva Veda* raises a banner of revolt on humanitarian grounds had already grown too old to be followed during the time which the *Ṛgveda* depicts. But although the old custom had been given up the the rites of its occasion, it would seem, still persisted and the procession of unwidowed women to adorn the widow for the company of the dead husband became one to deck her as a new bride. The process must have become very mechanical and sad for it is hardly human to be changed from a widow to a bride immediately after the death of the nearest relative and supporter of a woman even in the gay conditions of the Ṛg-vedic society.[214]

(3) *Yajur Veda*: *Taittirīya Saṁhitā*

The position regarding this passage is thus summed up by P.V. Kane:

> Raja Radhakant Deva relied upon two verses which he found in the Aukhya śākhā of the Tai. S. quoted in the 84th Anuvāka of the Nārāyaṇīya Upaniṣad as the most explicit authority for widow burning; *vide* Prof. H.H. Wilson's Works vol. II, pp. 293-305......These, to say the least, are of doubtful authenticity.[215]

(4) *Atharva Veda* XVIII-3-1

According to A.C. Das, the custom of self-immolation is referred to in the verse cited above.[216] The verse translates as follows:

> This woman, choosing her husband's world, lies down (*ni-pad*) by thee that art departed, O mortal, continuing to keep her ancient duty (*dharma*); to her assign thou here progeny and property.[217]

It is true that the commentator Sāyaṇa "declares that with this verse the wife is made to lie beside her dead husband on the funeral pile", but "the sense of (d) alone seems to indicate that the woman's action is nothing more than a show, expected to be followed by that of the next verse, since 'progeny and property' are rewards of this life, not for the other. The commentator says it is meant for her next birth."[218]

But the next verse, XVIII-3-2 is the same as the "verse in RV X.18.8", about which it has already been noticed and about which it may be reiterated that "the verse in consideration seems to be addressed by a priest to a wife who sat near the funeral pyre of her husband. Thus it proceeds: "Rise, come into the *world of life*. O woman ! come, he is lifeless by whose side thou liest. Wifehood with this thy husband was thy portion, who took thy hand and wooed thee as a lover." The word "*Jīvaloka*" in the verse is certainly enough to support the view that a widow was not consigned to flames but brought back to the living world to lead her life as usual."[219]

Hence, while it is clear that the custom of sati is alluded to in the Vedic verses, it is equally clear that it was not practised. In other words, the allusion to the existence of sati in the Vedas should not generate the illusion of its existence in Vedic times.

IV

To conclude: (1) *smṛti* literature seems to sanction sati but only in part, and (2) *śruti* literature does not seem to sanction it at all.

7

THE IDENTIFICATION OF A NEW FORM OF SATI

I

The word *suttee* or *sati*[220] has been part of the English language since the 18th century.[221] But the English word is a misnomer, not only because it applies the "substantive to the act instead of to the person",[222] but because it obscures the distinction between various forms of sati. In this essay an attempt will be made to identify a rare form of sati. Before this can be done, however, the various existing forms of sati now covered by that blanket term must be clearly indicated.

II

Sati, in Hindu usage, as pointed out earlier, is referred to as *sahamaraṇa* in the case of concremation and *anumaraṇa*[223] when the immolation occurs after the husband's cremation. The expressions *sahagamana* and *anugamana* are also used,[224] as also *anvārohaṇa* which rather graphically refers to the occasion "when the widow ascends the funeral pyre of her husband and is burnt along with the corpse".[225] Out of these various expressions *anumaraṇa* seems to be the one attested to most often in Sanskrit literature.[226]

It is clear from these various terms that sati could be committed at two points in time: either at the time of the husband's cremation or at some later point in time. There are even cases of sati being attempted almost a year after the husband's death.[227] In any case, however, these forms of sati come into play after the husband's death.

III

There is, however, another kind of sati attested to in *Harṣacarita*, the historical romance by Bāṇabhaṭṭa about his patron king Harṣavardhana composed in the seventh century A.D.[228] The fifth chapter of the *Harṣacarita* describes how the mother of Harṣa consigns herself to the flames in anticipation of her husband's (king Prabhākaravardhana's) death. When Prince Harṣa tries to dissuade her she remarks:

> I would die while still unwidowed. I cannot endure, like the widowed Rati, to make unavailing lamentations for a burnt husband.[229] Going before, like the dust of your father's feet, to announce his coming to the heavens, I shall be high esteemed of the hero-loving spouses of the gods. Nay, what will the smoke-bannered one[230] burn of me, who am already on fire with the sight of his heart-rending pains? Not to die, but to live at such a time would be unfeeling. Compared with the flame of wifely sorrow, whose fuel is imperishable love, fire itself is chilly cold. How suits it to be parsimonious of a life light as a bit of rotten straw, when the life's lord, majestic as Kailāśa, is passing away? Even should I live, yet after the mortal sin of slighting the king's death, the joys, my son, of my son's rule will touch me not. In those that are consumed by grief felicity is ominous, accursed and unavailing. Not in the body, dear son, but in the glory of loyal widows would I abide on earth. Therefore dishonour me no more, I beseech you, beloved son, with opposition to my heart's desire.[231]

And finally,

> Having embraced her son and kissed his head, the queen went forth on foot from the women's quarter, and, though the heavens, filled with the citizen's lamentations, seemed to block her path, proceeded to Sarasvatī's banks. Then, having worshipped the fire with the blooming red lotus posies of a woman's timorous glances, she plunged into it, as the moon's form enters the adorable sun.[232]

IV

It is clear that what queen Yaśomatī did does not fit the regular description of a sati, "this is not a proper case of *satī*, as she burnt herself even before her husband died".[233] It is, however, quite obvious that she looked upon herself as at least a would-be widow; indeed she indirectly refers to herself as one of the loyal widows (*viśvastānām vidhavānām*).[234]

It is therefore suggested that Yaśomatī's self-sacrifice be looked upon as a form of sati, indeed a unique form, but nevertheless a form of sati and that in Hindu terms such cases may be referred to as those of *Pūrvānumaraṇa*, notwithstanding the paradoxical connotation, which reflects the paradox of the situation itself.[235]

8

RAJA RAMMOHUN ROY (1772-1833) AND BAL GANGADHAR TILAK (1857-1920): A COMPARISON BASED ON ROY'S ATTITUDE TOWARDS SATI

I

In much of modern historiography about British India, Raja Rammohun Roy has the image of an ardent social reformer[236] and Bal Gangadhar Tilak at least that of a social conservative, if not that of a social reactionary.[237] While this essay does not set out to debate this issue, it aims at indicating that, notwithstanding their differences, both of these famous Indians seem to stand on the same platform in one remarkable respect. This becomes clear once their respective roles in the context of social reform are analyzed: that of Raja Rammohun Roy in the abolition of sati and that of Bal Gangadhar Tilak in the opposition to the Age of Consent Bill and Act, "which prohibited cohabitation before a wife reached the age of twelve".[238] The comparison is all the more significant because both these occasions represent landmarks in the social history of India.[239] When the respective roles of these two leaders are analyzed in detail, one discovers that their positions have, to a certain extent, been misrepresented and that in one crucial respect this double misrepresentation has had the effect of concealing a remarkable convergence.

II

Amidst the kudos which is showered on Raja Rammohun Roy for his role in the advocacy of the abolition of sati[240] one crucial fact is often overlooked: that when Lord William Bentinck sought his advice on the matter of the British prohibiting the practice of sati, he advised Lord William Bentinck *against* such a step.

This remarkable circumstance, however, must first be placed in its full perspective.

By 1828 Lord William Bentinck had ascertained the opinion of the judges and officers of the Government but had no way of ascertaining native Indian opinion on the question of abolition of sati. But he had heard of Rammohun Roy as an advocate of the abolition of sati and sought a meeting with him. The manner in which this came about was thus "narrated by Rev. Dr K.S. MacDonald, at a meeting in 1879, on the information supplied to him by Ananda Chandra Basu, the oldest pupil then living of Rammohun".[241]

> Lord William Bentinck, the Governor-General, on hearing that he would receive considerable help from the Raja in suppressing the pernicious custom of widow-burning, sent one of his *aides-de-camp* to him expressing his desire to see him. To this the Raja replied, "I have now given up all worldly avocations, and am engaged in religious culture and in the investigation of truth. Kindly express my humble respects to the Governor-General and inform him that I have no inclination to appear before his august presence, and therefore I hope that he will kindly pardon me". These words the *aide-de-camp* conveyed to the Governor-General, who enquired, "What did you say to Rammohun Roy?" The *aide-de-camp* replied, "I told him that Lord William Bentinck, the Governor-General, would be pleased to see him". The Governor-General answered, "Go back and tell him again that Mr William Bentinck will be highly obliged to him if he will kindly see him once". This the *aide-de-camp* did and Rammohun Roy could no longer refuse the urgent and polite request of his lordship.[242]

The meeting did take place and was noticed in the *Indian Gazette* of July 27, 1829 thus:

> An eminent native philanthropist who has long taken the lead of his countrymen on this great question has been encouraged to submit his views of it in a written form, and has been subsequently honoured with an audience by the Governor-General, who, we learn, has expressed his anxious desire to put an end to a custom constituting so foul a blot.[243]

Now what transpired at this meeting? Lord William Bentinck provides us with a gist of the discussion himself. He first refers to the views of Mr Horace Wilson, that once the Indians-through the suppression of sati-begin to suspect, "that it is the intention of the British Government to abandon this hitherto inviolate principle of allowing the most complete toleration in matters of religion that there will arise in the minds of all so deep a distrust of our ulterior designs that they will no longer be tractable to any arrangement intended for their improvement, and that the principle of a purer morality, as well as of a more virtuous and exalted rule of action, now actually inculcated by European education and knowledge, will receive a fatal check".[244] Then he goes on to say:

> I must acknowledge that a similar opinion as to the probable excitation of a deep distrust of our future intentions was mentioned to me in a conversation by that enlightened native, Rammohun Roy, a warm advocate for the abolition of *Sati* and of all other superstitions and corruptions engrafted on Hindu religion, which he considers originally to have been a pure Deism. It was his opinion that the practice might be suppressed quietly and unobservedly by increasing the difficulties and by the indirect agency of the police. He apprehended that any public enactment would give rise to general apprehension, that the reasoning would be, while the English were contending for power they deemed it politic to allow universal toleration and to respect our religion, but having obtained the supremacy their first act is a violation of their profession, and the next will probably be, like the Muhammadan conquerors, to force upon us their own religion.[245]

It is clear, therefore, that while Raja Rammohun Roy advocated the abolition of sati, *he did not approve of this being done by the British Government directly*. He did not approve of British governmental interference in the sphere of Hindu social life.

Thus while Raja Rammohun Roy's meeting with Lord William Bentinck was cordial, it was marked by a difference of opinion. However, once[246] Lord William Bentinck took the action of abolishing sati, Raja Rammohun Roy came out in open support for it.[247]

Thus Raja Rammohun Roy's attitude on the point of British government interference in Hindu social life may be described as one of ex-ante objection but ex-post approbation.

III

We may now turn to the role of Bal Gangadhar Tilak in the controversy surrounding the Age of Consent Bill. It was also a humanitarian piece of legislation like the abolition of sati, its presentation to the Legislative Council being precipitated "in 1890 with the death of eleven-year-old Phulmani Bai in Calcutta, from lacerations she received during intercourse". It may be noted that Bal Gangadhar Tilak objected to the measure *publicly* on the same ground on which Raja Rammohun Roy had objected *privately* to the abolition of sati. He wrote:

> We would not like that Government should have anything to do with regulating our social customs or ways of living, even supposing that the act of Government will be a very beneficial and suitable measure.[248]

Also, like Raja Rammohun Roy, he referred to Muslim rule:

> This we have to admit if we look at the Age of Consent Bill. The Muhammadans forced the Hindus to grow beards after cutting off Hindus' locks of hair by taking a sword in one hand and a Koran in the other. So also our subjugation to others gives evidence that our brave English people have the power to send us to "Our Father in Heaven" after making us drink red water (wine) instead of the sacred water of the Ganges.[249]

It should be recalled here that "he performed the marriage of his daughters after they had attained the age of sixteen".[250] In doing so he was not conforming to the Age of Consent Act but to his own suggestion of voluntary agreement among Hindus to raise the minimum age of marriage in Hindu society.[251]

It is clear, therefore, that there is a basic identity in approach adopted by both Raja Rammohun Roy and Bal Gangadhar Tilak on the issue of British governmental interference in Hindu social life.[252]

IV

There were, however, differences in detail—differences in biographical and political detail. Some of these may be quickly noted.

(1) The cordiality which surrounded Raja Rammohun Roy's association with the British Government is conspicuous by its absence in the case of Bal Gangadhar Tilak[253] (who was imprisoned by the British).[254]

This difference in detail fits into another pattern—that of altered Indo-British relations between the eighteenth and the nineteenth centuries.[255]

(2) Raja Rammohun Roy came out on the side of the British after sati was abolished by a governmental fiat, though he had advised against such a measure. Bal Gangadhar Tilak did not follow suit. "Even after the Bill was passed, he moved a resolution in the Bombay Provincial Social Reform Committee in May 1891 condemning the Government for not respecting legitimately and widely expressed public opinion and no one dared oppose the resolution. It was even resolved that Parliament should be moved to repeal the legislation but the movement slowly subsided and died down".[256]

(3) Raja Rammohun Roy never made a *public* issue of governmental interference in Hindu life. Bal Gangadhar Tilak did.[257]

This again corresponds to another pattern—the change in Indian attitude towards the British Government and the public expression thereof, after the founding of the Indian National Congress.[258]

(4) The role of both Raja Rammohun Roy and Bal Gangadhar Tialk also seems to correspond to their vision of the future of British rule in India. Although both swore by British Raj,[259] for Raja Rammohun Roy the prospect of the termination of British rule in India lay in the distant future indeed, British rule was just starting in right earnest in his time. He witnessed only the end of the beginning of British Rule in India. But Bal Gangadhar Tilak had perhaps begun to sense the beginning of the end of British rule.[260] These outlooks seem to have influenced the degree of vigour and determination they decided to bring to bear on their disapproval of British governmental interference in Hindu life.

(5) It also needs to be considered that while in the case of Rammohun Roy, his interest in the abolition of sati *preceded* effective governmental concern with the issue,[261] Bal Gangadhar Tilak's interest seems to have arisen *because* of governmental concern with the issue.[262] Between the questions of reform of Hindu society and the preservation of its integrity, on the face of it, the former seems to have been closer to Raja Rammohun Roy's heart, the latter to Bal Gangadhar Tilak's. However, it must be borne in mind that by Bal Gangadhar Tilak's time the notion of self-government by Indians had taken shape, while Raja Rammohun Roy was grateful that British rule had supplanted Muslim rule ![263] Bal Gangadhar wanted that self-government to *precede* any further reform of Hindu society.[264]

V

It is clear, however, that in spite of these personal and contextual differences both Raja Rammohun Roy and Bal Gangadhar Tilak seem to share one fundamental conviction: That the reform of Hindu society is the responsibility of the Hindus and not of non-Hindus. This convergence in their conviction is often not recognized. It was the purpose of this essay to spotlight it.

9

WIDOWS ARE NOT FOR BURNING : NATIVE RESPONSE TO THE ABOLITION OF THE SATI RITE

The Hindu practice of burning widows alive, or, the sati rite as it is known, was abolished by regulation XVII of 1829 (December 4). The *Calcutta Gazette* in its editorial congratulated the native and European inhabitants for this achievement and hoped to have no more "of those baneful sacrifices". Though Lord Bentinck deserves the main credit for the legislation, the abolition marked the successful culmination of the efforts of many others—Muslim rulers like Akbar and Jahangir, the Sikh Guru Amardas, the Maratha chief Ahalya Bai, the ruler of Tanjore, the Peshwa Balaji Rao, Albuquerque of Goa, etc., and in the British period Government officials, British public opinion and Christian missionaries. But the native response in favour of abolition, which grew up in the early 19th century, and worked as a very effective force from inside the community, is not yet appreciated fully. They disputed the orthodox claim that the sati rite was a part of Hindu religion, gave a rationalistic interpretation of the scriptures, and even under the threat of excommunication pleaded for its abolition. We know of them from the *Friend of India*, the *Calcutta Gazette*, the *Bengal Harkaru*, the *Samacara Darpana*, and the *Samacara Candrika*, from British Parliamentary papers, from the speech of John Poynder at the Courts of the Proprietors of East India Stock, and from the Bentinck papers. Nearly nine years before Bentinck's regulation, the *Calcutta Journal* wrote—"It is more than gratifying to find, that while the British population in India are generally speaking indifferent to the subject there has arisen among the Hindoos themselves a powerful opposition to the continuation of these barbarous murders, and that great learning, talent, ingenuity and moral courage have been displayed by those who endeavour to prove that even by the Hindoo laws such sacrifices are not binding; and who strenuously labour to effect their abolition".[265]

Between 1815 and 1817, the number of widows burnt alive in the three Presidencies of Bengal, Bombay and Fort St George, was 1527 (British Parliamentary Paper), 95% of which were in Bengal. While the orthodox Hindus claimed religious sanction for the rite and proclaimed it as an act of great spiritual merit, and while the humanitarians everywhere were clamouring for its abolition, the government of the time, reluctant to interfere with religious beliefs of the Hindus, and apprehensive of disturbances which such interference might spark off, was in a dilemma and remained fairly inactive. There was a stalemate, and Brahmin priests, apprehending some restrictions on the rite from the government, became overenthusiastic in their religious duties and the number of satis continued increasing. Then in 1817 came a breakthrough.

Mṛtyuñjaya Vidyālaṅkāra, a Brahmin of profound scholarship and of high respectability in the community, who, according to John Clark Marshman "bore a strong resemblance to our great lexicographer (Dr Johnson) not only by his stupendous acquirements and soundness of his critical judgement but also in his rough features and unwieldy figure",[266] declared, after analysing the views held by different schools of Hindu law, that it was not specially enjoined in the Hindu *śāstra* that the widow must burn herself, and that the sati rite was purely voluntary, and not an ordinance of the *śāstra*. He concluded, "I regard a woman's burning herself as an unworthy act, and a life of abstinence and chastity as highly excellent". He further added, "No blame whatever is attached to those who prevent a woman's burning".[267] Mṛtyuñjaya's comment was probably the most effective single argument for the abolition of the rite. On the one hand it wrecked the orthodox claim of religious sanction, and on the other it gave the hesitant government positive encouragement for abolition. Twelve years later Bentinck echoed Mṛtyuñjaya's words in his regulation-"it is nowhere enjoined by the religion of the Hindoos as an imperative duty, on the contrary a life of purity and retirement on the part of the widow is more especially and preferably inculcated."[268]

Mṛtyuñjaya's method of interpretation followed the Indian logical tradition that in the case of a conflict the lower authority should always give way to the higher. The *Śruti* (i.e. Vedic literature) should prevail over the *Smṛti*, and in *Smṛti*, which contains the Hindu laws, the ordinance of the senior law makers should always prevail over the minor ones. Manu should prevail over Yājñavalkya, and Yājñavalkya over Aṅgiras, Hārīta, Bṛhaspati, etc. Mṛtyuñjaya's comment on the legality of the rite was based on such a comparative evaluation. Though he was never an active supporter of abolition, his comment provided the opponents of the rite with the most effective weapon in their fight for abolition.

Mṛtyuñjaya's interpretation of Hindu law on sati was well utilized by Rammohun Roy, who, unlike Mṛtyuñjaya, was an active participant in the issue. It might be that his involvement was not purely on humanitarian grounds, but also had some utilitarian motive. As a humanitarian he felt for the unfortunate widows and pleaded for the abolition of the rite. As a utilitarian, he wanted to gain some indirect advantages which might come out of the abolition for his countrymen, particularly for the native business community. In the early 19th century his community was not in a very happy situation. Up to now they had acted as the middlemen between the East India Company and the local producers of raw goods, but with the Company's new policy of dealing direct with local producers, the business of the community was threatened. As their representative, Rammohun voiced their grievances, supported free trade against the monopoly of the Company and asked the authorities for greater facilities in business and certain social and political advantages. But were the Indians capable of handling the advantages they were asking for? Lord Cornwallis had already branded them as corrupt, and according to Macaulay, perjury and forgery formed an integral part of their character, and though there were a few kind words from Walter Hamilton and Maria Graham, the native religion with practices like sati, seemed to be a stumbling block to achieving a better image for them. So something should be done about religion "for the sake of their political advantage and social comfort",[269] and Rammohun appeared as a reformer. He wrote two pamphlets favouring abolition, publicised the issue widely and organised a group of opponents to the rite. The pamphlets were directed not only to his countrymen but also "to alter the notions that some European gentlemen entertain on the subject."[270] With his deep knowledge of the *śāstra*, he quoted from Manu, Yājñavalkya, Viṣṇu, Vasiṣṭha, the *Bhagavadgītā*, etc., and showed that the rite of burning widows alive not only had no sanction of the higher authorities but also was contrary to their dictates. Did not the *Kena-upaniṣad* say that rites which had future reward for their object were inferior religious practices? Did not the *Muṇḍaka-upaniṣad* proclaim that "those fools who immersed in the foolish practice of rites, consider themselves too wise and learned, are repeatedly subjected to birth, disease, death and other pains?" The great Manu had directed Hindu widows live as ascetics. If custom or long tradition ought to set aside the precepts of the *śāstra*, and should be the determining factor, as the advocates of the rite claimed, then "the inhabitants of the forests and mountains who have been in the habit of plunder, must be considered as guiltless of sin, and it would be improper to endeavour to restrain their habits". We had our *śāstra*, and we had our reason. In the *śāstra* such female murder was altogether forbidden, and our reason also declared "that to bind a woman for her destruction, holding out to her the inducement of heavenly rewards, is a most sinful act".[271]

Rammohun's argument was clear, logical and forceful, and his contribution towards abolition was no doubt great, but he was hesitant to abolish the practice by government legislation. Bentinck wrote in his minute of 8 November 1929—"It was his opinion that the practice might be suppressed quietly and unobservedly by increasing the difficulties...He apprehended that any public enactment would give rise to general apprehension".[272] It might be that Rammohun misjudged the feeling of his countrymen on sati, but it was more probable that he himself was reluctant to see any direct outside interference with the Hindu religion. In their history of political turmoils and cultural crises, the Hindus had jealously guarded their religion and were always apprehensive of interference from the ruling power. In the British period, the crude preaching of some of the missionaries and their over-enthusiasm for conversion did not alleviate this fear. If Rammohun was reluctant to agree to legislation for abolition, it was because he did not think it wise to establish a precedent for interference. But once the law was passed he supported it whole-heartedly.

One of the followers of Rammohun in his movement for abolition was Gourisankara Bhattacarya, the editor of a Bengali weekly *Sambada Bhaskara.* He was an independent and forceful writer and a keen supporter of widow remarriage and girls' education. The *Calcutta Courier* wrote about him: "Being freed from his trammels of Hindoo superstition, he gladly embraces every opportunity of exposing the folly of his bigoted countrymen". Gourisankara went to Government House, pleaded with Bentinck for the abolition of the rite and was threatened by its advocates with excommunication from society. Long afterwards, he wrote in one of his editorials "If I could oppose directly and without fear the big bosses of society in advocating the abolition of concremation, then nothing would deter me from expressing myself freely."[273]

Gourisankara was not excommunicated, but Kalinath Roy Chowdhury "of one of the most ancient and honourable families in Bengal" was not so fortunate. He and his associates were expelled from Hindu society in Calcutta and it was decided "that they are not to be invited to any festivals, marriages, or funeral obsequies".[274] Kalinath was an active supporter for abolition and when the regulation was passed he led a delegation of Hindu inhabitants to congratulate Lord Bentinck.

Other names worth mentioning in the anti-sati movement were those of Dwarakanath Tagore and Prasanna Kumar Tagore —two prominent businessmen of Calcutta, Munshi Mathuranath Mullick, Ramakrishna Sinha, and Anandaprasad Bandyopadhyay. Bishop Heber quoted Mr Marshman—"...among the laity many powerful and wealthy persons agree, and publicly express their agreement, with Rammohun Roy, in reprobating the custom".[275] A vigorous press campaign against the sati rite was also launched through three journals—the *Sambada Kawmudi*, the *Samacara Darpana*, and the *Bangadoot*, and by 1826 the attention of the English-educated Bengali youth was drawn to the subject. Letters appeared in the *Bengal Hurkaru* (30 January 1826 and 1 February 1826) denouncing the sati rite and all those who encouraged it, and calling upon the Government to take effective measures to prevent the practice.

So in the first half of the 19th century, just before Bentinck introduced his regulation, there were, in the Hindu community, a group of advocates for the sati rite, a group of opponents to the rite, and a non-committed group—the "silent majority"—who were rather indifferent to the whole issue. The indifference of this "silent majority" worked in both ways—indifference to the arguments of the opponents to the rite, and indifference to the appeal of the orthodox leaders to save a Hindu rite. The first one was the effect of insensibility caused "by witnessing from your youth the voluntary burning of women among your elder relatives, your neighbours and the inhabitants of the surrounding villages, and by observing the indifference at the time when the women are writhing under the torture of the flames..."[276] And the second one was caused by the impact of the liberal tradition of mediaeval India, which questioned the validity of meaningless ceremonialism in religion and denounced the autocracy of the priests. This was the tradition of Ramananda, Kabir, Dadu and Nanak. Some of the schools of this tradition had a large number of followers throughout India, and the social and religious ideas of some were progressive even by modern standards. They were responsible, at least to some extent, for defusing in the common people the sense of anger which might have been produced otherwise by interference with their religious rites from outside. Cases where local natives helped the government officials to prevent the rite were not uncommon, and the *Friend of India* calculated "on the support of all the humane, the wise, and the good through India" for abolition. They also mentioned those "who used all their powers and influences to liberate their country from the stigma of this guilt by preventing their own mothers and sisters from ascending the funeral pile".

In 1828 Lord Bentinck reached India as Governor-General. He still had vivid memories of the Vellore mutiny and his inglorious departure from Madras in 1807, and the remarks made about him in the Court of Directors' letters were still ringing in his ears—"after weighing all the considerations connected with the business of Vellore, we felt ourselves unable longer to continue that confidence to him which it is so necessary for a person holding his situation to possess."[277] Yet Bentinck had no illusions about the sati rite, and he had no hesitation in abolishing it.

On 12 June 1829 he wrote to Astell, the Chairman of the Board of Directors, East India Company—"There cannot be a man more anxious for the abolition of that horrible rite than myself. I do not believe that among the most anxious advocates of that measure any one of them feel more deeply than I do, the dreadful responsibility hanging over my happiness in this world and the next, if, as the Governor-General of India, I was to consent to the continuance of that practice for one minute longer".[278] And the agony of a humanitarian gradually turned into the determination of an administrator.

Bentinck recognised in his minute of 8 November 1829 the support given to him and to the cause of abolition by different sections of the Indian population, namely the judges of the Nizamat Adalat, the police superintendents, the various public functionaries, military officers and others. He concluded—"I write and feel as a legislator for the Hindus, and as I believe many enlightened Hindus think and feel." Bentinck realised that it would be foolish even of a man with bitter memories of Vellore to miss the opportunity while a strong native response for abolition was sweeping over the country. And he acted. Frederick John Shore in his *Notes on Indian Affairs* wrote afterwards that the tide of opinion in India was so strongly opposed to sati rite that any Governor-General would have acted as Bentinck did.[279]

The regulation for abolition did bring some protests from the orthodox, but it caused no serious trouble as the Government anticipated. Instead, 1,100 Calcutta residents (300 Hindus among them) sent congratulatory letters to Lord Bentinck and the poet Derozio wrote:

> Back to its cavern ebbs the tide of crime,
> There fettered, locked, and powerless it sleeps;
> And History bending o'er the page of Time,
> Where many a mournful record still she keeps,
> The widowed Hindu's fate no longer weeps;
> The priestly tyrant's cruel chain is broken
> And to the den alarmed the monster creeps,
> The charm that mars his mystic spell is spoken.

In more recent days some scholars have tried to justify the

institution of sati, probably for the sake of novelty. Ananda Kentish Coomaraswamy in his *Sati: a vindication of the Hindu woman,* a paper read before the Sociological Society in London (on November 12, 1912) provided a philosophical justification of the rite. With examples of Hindu women burning themselves happily with their dead husbands, Coomaraswamy talked about the high ideals of Eastern women which he thought were quite different from not only the ideal of Western women but also those of Eastern men. And so when, out of devotion, wives died on their husbands' funeral pyres, husbands, with their different ideals, were not required to go through a similar process. John Rosetti (University of Sussex) in his Anandilal Poddar lectures entitled *Lord William Bentinck and His Age* mentioned some American historians who were rather kind to the rite. Talking about the abolition he said—"in itself (the abolition) is thought of as a Good Thing by everybody except some American historians whose own great-grandmothers were not involved".[280]

Since the Regulation, the practice of widow-burning was a lost cause for the orthodox, a dead issue for the public, and a subject of the past for the historians. In a narrow view the rite was an Indian practice, but in a wider view it was the local development of a custom practised in some form or other over a wide area of the world—in Slavonic lands, Scandinavia, Greece, Egypt, China, etc.[281] The original cause of the custom might be the jealousy of men over women. The native opponents to the sati rite pointed out that the cause of such a practice was—"Excessive jealousy of their female connections operating in the breasts of Hindoo Princes...They availed themselves of their arbitrary power, and under the cloak of religion introduced the practice of burning widows alive...".[282]

Jealous men once invented the chastity belt for their wives to wear when they went on long journeys. But for the longest journey—the journey to eternity from where there is no return—they decided to take their wives with them so that they could rest in peace in their tombs.

10

WIDOWS ARE NOT FOR BURNING: CHRISTIAN MISSIONARY PARTICIPATION IN THE ABOLITION OF THE SATI RITE

All missionaries did not feel it proper to involve themselves deeply in the religious beliefs of the Hindus and to plead for the abolition of the sati rite. Abbe Jean Antoine Dubois (1765-1848) who described in detail the burning of the two widows of the last King of Tanjore (died in 1801), was at a loss to find any reasons for such 'superstitious fanaticism'. In his *Hindu manners, customs and ceremonies* he wrote: "It is indeed unaccountable how these Brahmins, who are so scrupulous and attach so much importance to the life of the most insignificant insect, and whose feelings are excited to pity and indignation at the very sight of a cow being slaughtered, can, with such savage coldbloodedness and wicked satisfaction, look upon so many weak and innocent human beings".[283] But it was with the advent of the Protestant missionaries at the end of the century, that the movement for the abolition of the sati rite began in earnest.

The Christian missionary involvement for the abolition of the sati rite was only an offshoot of their grand design in India which was conversion of the country to Christianity. Rev. Claudius Buchanan of the Church of England, who landed in Bengal in 1790, had no illusions about such success. In his sermon 'Eras of light',[284] he divided human history since the beginning of Christianity into three eras—(1) the first era was that of the promulgation of the Gospel by Christ himself; (2) the second was the era of reformation, and (3) the third era of light is the present period when Christianity has assumed its true character as "Light of the World". The Holy Scriptures are multiplying without number and preachers are going forth into almost every region "to make the ways of God known upon earth".[285] So as a historical process, Christianity was bound to come to a heathen land like India. But the process of preaching the works of the Gospel to the natives, to convince them of the superiority of the Bible, and convert them to Christianity was a lengthy affair. There were already certain superstitions in Indian society, as the missionaries saw them, which needed urgent attention and which should be dealt with at once. There were those practices or rituals which inflicted immediate death or tended to produce death. One of these practices was the rite of sati. Buchanan advocated abolition of the rite by law and argued that when the practice of sacrificing children—another "bloody superstition" of the Hindus—had been abolished by Wellesley by the Regulation VI of 1802, "not a murmur followed", and that there would neither be any if the Government abolished the sati rite by a regulation. Moreover, the Pundits and chief Brahmins of the College of Fort William had intimated "that if government will pass a regulation, amercing by fine every Brahmin who attends a burning, or every Zamindar who permits him to attend it, the practice cannot possibly long continue".[286] He hoped that the civilized world might expect soon to hear of the abolition of "this opprobrium of a Christian administration, the female sacrifice".[287]

In November 1793 Rev. William Carey of the Baptist Mission arrived at Calcutta. After nearly six years in the spring of 1799, he saw widow-burning one evening. It was in a place thirty miles away from Calcutta. He tried to stop the ceremony and to reason with the widow and the Brahmin priests. "I talked till reasoning was of no use, and then began to exclaim with all my might against what they were doing, telling them it was shocking murder. They told me it was a great act of holiness".[288] Carey was greatly agitated, his spirit was in anguish, and "he vowed like Lincoln later concerning the auction of slave women 'to hit this accursed thing hard', if God should spare him".[289] Carey started immediately. He sent careful investigators to every village within a radius of thirty miles of Calcutta, to learn how many widows had been immolated there in the previous twelve months, and their ages, and the children they had left behind them. "Four hundred and thirty-eight was the damning total in this specific area alone, the toll of a single year's superstition, cruelty and waste".[290] The Serampore Missionaries under the leadership of Carey implored the Government to forbid the rite by law. Carey made use of his position as a lecturer in the College of Fort William to collect from the pundits there various texts from the Hindu *śāstras* on which the practice of sati was allegedly based. The missionaries placed all these documents together with the statistics of sati they had already compiled, in the hands of George Udney—a member of the Supreme Council and an ardent abolitionist. Udney's submission on sati was "the first official notice regarding female immolation which had appeared in the records of Government".[291] As a result Wellesley's Government asked the judges of the Nizamat Adalat to "ascertain in the first instance, by means of a reference to the pundits how far the practice above noticed (*sati*) is founded on the religious opinion of the Hindoos".[292] But Lord Wellesley's reign was ending, and with a swarm of critics in London and in Calcutta, he feared to risk a reform so challenged and so controversial.

Reginald Heber, the second Protestant Bishop of Calcutta, was concerned with the burning of the widows, but he took a rather academic interest in the subject. One day while returning from Calcutta he saw a funeral pile on which a widow was just burnt with her dead husband. "I felt very sick at heart and regretted I had not been half an hour sooner".[293] He tried to determine the prescribed position of the woman on a funeral pyre, whether the widow was laid below the dead body of her husband as happened in this case of burning which he witnessed, or was laid by the side of the dead body as the missionaries described in their account of the sati rite. Heber was very appreciative of the work for abolition already done by the Baptist missionaries. He invited Joshua Marshman from Serampore ("Dr Carey is too lame to go out"), expressed his concern about widow-burning, and asked Marshman's opinion on the possibility of abolition. Marshman informed him that these 'horrors' were of more frequent occurrence within these last few years than when he first knew Bengal. The increase according to him, might be due to the increasing luxury of the higher and middle classes, and "to their expensive imitation of European habits which makes many families needy, and anxious to get rid, by any means, of the necessity of supporting their mothers, or the widow of their relations."[294] Another cause might be the jealousy of old men with young wives, who even in death, tried to cling to their exclusive possession. Marshman was strongly of the opinion that the practice might be forbidden "without exciting any serious murmurs".[295] The reason for such opinion was that the Brahmin priests had no longer the power and popularity they once had and "among the laity many powerful and wealthy persons agree, and publicly express their agreement, with Rammohun Roy, in reprobating the custom, which is now well known to be not commanded by any of the Hindoo sacred books".[296] The senior judge of the Sadar Dewani Adalat also gave a similar opinion on abolition. On the other hand, some of the members of the Government with whom Heber discussed the issue "think differently". They argued that the present restriction on the rite forbade any woman to be burnt without her own wish certified to the magistrate, but if the rite was forbidden by law there were other and less public ways to die which might be resorted to. Moreover, if the missionaries wanted to convert the Hindus it was better for them to keep the Government entirely out of sight. The solution of the problem probably lay in Christian education. "When Christian schools have become universal the suttee will fall of itself".[297] But to forbid it by any legislative enactment would, in their opinion "only give currency to the notion that we mean to impose Christianity on them by force".[298]

The Christian missionaries tried to mould the public opinion against the sati rite in both India and Britain. In Britain, Claudius Buchanan's widely-read *Christian Researches in India* (published in 1811) gave the number of widows burnt on the funeral pyres of their husbands, and William Wilberforce quoted the statistics of satis which the Baptist missionaries compiled, in the House of Commons on June 22, 1813. The occasion of the debate was the renewal of the Company's charter and the theme of his speech was the propagation of Christianity in India. He mentioned that in the radius of 30 miles around Calcutta, 130 widows were burnt in six months. In the year 1803, within the same space, the number amounted to 275, "one of whom was a girl of eleven years of age". He also mentioned an incident of sati witnessed by Marshman who thus concluded his dreadful experience—"To have seen savage wolves thus tearing a human body, limb from limb, would have been shocking; but to see relations and neighbours do this to one with whom they had familiarly conversed not an hour before, and to do it with an air of levity, was almost too much for me to bear".[299] Two missionary journals—The *Missionary Register* and the *Missionary Papers* circulated a series of authentic records of sati forwarded by the missionaries in India, and the *Missionary Papers* in particular emphasized the horror of the ceremony with its vivid engravings of widows about to cast themselves into the flames.[300] In 1810 William Ward published his *History, Literature, and Mythology of the Hindoos* (renamed afterwards *A View of the History, Literature and Religion of the Hindoos*). In it Ward described some incidents of widow-burning with comments like "most shocking and atrocious murder".[301] In 1818 when Ward went to England he confirmed his accounts of widow-burning, and in 1821, on his way back to India he wrote *Farewell Letters* to friends in England and America which he subsequently published. In these letters he presented a picture of "the superstitions of the natives, the impunity and cruelty to which they gave birth, and the moral and religious degradation they entailed".[302] On the subject of widow-burning his letters were dramatic and effective—"O that I could collect all the shrieks of these affrighted victims, all the innocent blood thus drunk up by the devouring element, and all the wailings of thirteen thousand orphans".[303] James Pegg, a former missionary of Cuttack published his *India's Cries to British Humanity*.[304] In the Parliament Mr Fowell Buxton moved for publication of copies or extracts of all communications from India, respecting the burning of females on the funeral piles of their husbands. On the subject of abolition he said that he was aware that a feeling of delicacy upon the superstition of the natives alone restricted the British authorities from interfering to prevent these dreadful spectacles. Still the question was not, in fact, one of religious toleration, but whether murder and suicide ought tacitly to be permitted under British jurisdiction.

Stirred by the public interest which the missionaries had aroused by their publicity, and anxious to terminate the rite without causing much unrest among the Hindus, the Parliament, the Board of Control, and the British people became more concerned with the issue.

The abolition of the sati rite in 1829 owes much to the efforts of the Christian missionaries. Under the watchful eye of a Government which was hesitant to take any action to terminate the rite, and reluctant to allow missionary interference in the religious beliefs of the Hindus, and in the face of rather cold indifference of the native people, the missionaries started working for the abolition of a practice which they thought inhuman. They sent investigators, collected data and compiled statistics of the victims, and they preached and published books and pamphlets against the rite, and thus helped to create in Britain an anti-sati public opinion which eventually forced the issue before the British Parliament. In India, the implied assertion of the missionaries that evil religious practices could only be the offshoots of an evil religion, and their criticism of Hinduism as the cause of rites like sati, stirred the otherwise passive and placid life of the nineteenth century Hindus. The missionary criticism of their religion produced among the Hindus two types of reaction— (a) religious conservatism which denied that there could be anything wrong in the religion and its rites and rituals, and (b) religious rationalism which thought it proper to re-examine the basic fundamentals of the religion and the rites and rituals which have gathered round it through the ages. The first reaction resulted in the *Dharma Sabha* of the orthodox Hindus who tried to retain the practice as an ancient tradition of the country, while as a result of the second there grew an antipathy towards the rite among certain sections of the Hindus who organised themselves against the rite. It was the response of this later group which helped Bentinck a great deal to make his final decision for abolition.

In the major part of the eighteenth century Christian missionaries in India, though disturbed by the inhumanity of the sati rite, did not set out to stop it, and the Court of Directors felt that it would be wise to rely on the man in the field—the Governor-General—for decision and proper action for the abolition.

In India, the criticism of the Christian missionaries brought the religion and customs of the Hindus into the open and exposed them for scrutiny. This sudden outside interference disturbed the otherwise placid life on the 19th century Hindus, and brought a great commotion in the native society which was consequently split up into two distinct groups—one for reform, and the other against it.

In 1817, Mṛtyuñjaya Vidyālaṅkāra, a Brahmin of profound scholarship and high respectability in the community, declared that the sati rite was not an ordinance of Hindu law, and a woman's burning herself as an unworthy act, and a life of abstinence and chastity as highly excellent for a widow.[305] Mṛtyuñjaya was a friend and colleague of William Carey. He was the chief pundit of Bengali and Sanskrit under Carey in the College of Fort William. He was also Carey's teacher. Mr Carey sat under his instructions two or three hours daily when in Calcutta, and the effect of this intercourse was speedily visible in the superior accuracy and purity of his translations.[306] It might be quite possible that Mṛtyuñjaya was sympathetic to Carey's concern over the sati rite. A year later Rammohun Roy utilized Mṛtyuñjaya's interpretation of Hindu law on sati, and built up for the first time an organised movement of resistance against the rite. The orthodox Hindus also organised themselves "for protecting our religion and our excellent customs and usage",[307] under the leadership of Radhakanta Deb.

In 1828 Lord Bentinck reached India as Governor-General. He was aware that both the Directors and Parliament actively desired the discontinuance of sati, and that section of the English public which took any interest in Indian affairs would support him in his measure to suppress the sati rite, which became a moral responsibility of the Government and a physical possibility, as various reports from India suggested. The memories of the Vellore mutiny and his inglorious departure from Madras also prompted him to perform some "good deeds" in India which might clear him of the blame for the mutiny and remove the disgrace which the letter of the Directors imputed. Above all, he himself was determined to abolish the rite—"There cannot be a man more anxious for the abolition of that horrible rite than myself".[308]

The Regulation XVII of 1829 abolished the sati rite with minor protest from the orthodox Hindus, and "for the first time during twenty centuries...the Ganges flowed unblooded to the sea".[309] Bentinck got his share of the credit for the abolition, Rammohun also got his, but somehow the missionaries were not mentioned much about their contribution to the reform. Bentinck did not mention them in his minute on sati, and Fanny

Parkes in her *Wanderings of a Pilgrim* bluntly denied any missionary participation—"The missionaries had nothing to do with it".[310] The reason for such omission might be due to the apprehension that the missionary participation in the reform was not an end by itself, but only a means to achieve their aim. The missionary idea of reform was not to make the society or religion better by the removal of imperfections, faults or errors which had crept into it, but to eliminate the imperfections, etc. with the ultimate aim of changing the religion and reorganising society. So it seems there was a difference in attitude to reform between the missionaries and Bentinck who wrote in his minute "The first and primary object of my heart is the benefit of the Hindus".[311] Another reason might be the poor image of the missionaries in India which overshadowed the humanitarian aspect of their labour. Overenthusiasm for conversion, imperfect knowledge of native religion and superficial knowledge of their own, lack of understanding and a crude way of preaching were some of the factors responsible for depicting the missionaries as a 'comic figure'. Maria Graham, writing about the Hindus in her *Letters on India*, pointed out emphatically that "never will a conversion be wrought among them by the present system of missionaries".[312] Rammohun Roy made fun out of them in his *A Dialogue Between a Missionary and Three Chinese Converts*, and Major-General Sleeman told us of Father Gregory's serious problem of converting the Hindus because the miraculous acts of Krishna far surpassed the miracles of Jesus.[313]

Yet to an independent observer of Indian history, the contribution of the missionaries to India's social and religious reforms cannot be overlooked. From the fortified social and religious system of the Hindus, they brought the sati issue out in the open and pointed out the inhumanity and insensibility of the whole community and appealed to stop a practice which was founded on stagnant and misguided ideas and false hopes. It was the missionaries who kept the issue alive in the conscience of the people in both India and Britain and it was they who helped indirectly to organise a Hindu response for abolition which as an internal force played an important part for the termination of the rite.

Now, nearly one-and-a-half centuries after the abolition, when the blue Indian sky is no more clouded by the black smoke from the sati funeral pyre, and the quiet river banks are no more disturbed by the deafening sound of the drums for the rite, a thinking Hindu should feel himself fortunate for not "witnessing from your youth the voluntary burning of women among your elder relatives, your neighbours, and the inhabitants of the surrounding villages, and by observing the indifference at the time when the women are writhing under the torture of the flames".[314] He should, no doubt, thank Bentinck for his great act of humanity. It would be fair for him to remember the missionaries also and thank them too.

11

THE BHAGAVADGĪTĀ: ITS ROLE IN THE ABOLITION OF SATI

I

It is well-known that the practice of widows burning themselves on the funeral pyre of their dead husband, known as sati,[315] was prevalent in Bengal in the nineteenth century,[316] till it was abolished by the British Governor-General William Bentinck on December 4, 1829.[317] It is also fairly well-known that Raja Rammohun Roy (1772-1833) campaigned vigorously for the abolition of this practice on the Indian side and was consulted by the Governor-General prior to the promulgation of the ordinance which had the effect of banning it.[318] It is, however, virtually unknown that Roy drew upon the *Bhagavadgītā*, among other texts, in presenting his case against the practice to his coreligionists. The purpose of this essay is to shed light on this little known fact about this well-known scripture.[319] The fact that its role in this respect has not hitherto come to light is perhaps to be accounted for by the fact that many scholars see the *Bhagavadgītā* as assuming prominence as a scripture within Hinduism only in the *latter* part of the nineteenth century.[320]

II

Roy cites no less than thirteen verses, one line and one hemistich from the *Bhagavadgītā* in building up the case against sati.[321] In order to fully appreciate his use of the *Gītā* in this context, it is necessary to state first the traditional aıgument in favour of sati.

Those Smṛti texts[322] which recommend sati (the *Manusmṛti* being a striking exception), do so on the argument that thereby heaven is secured by the widow. Roy counters this by invoking the doctrine of *niṣkāma karma* of the *Gītā*,[323] namely that action performed without desire for reward is superior to one directed towards it and hence to be preferred. As sati is a reward-oriented act, aimed at securing residence in heaven, it is an inferior form of action and therefore to be discouraged. The following verses are cited by Roy in support of his position. Roy provides his own translations, I have followed Franklin Edgerton.

> For action is far inferior
> To discipline of mental attitude, Dhanaṁjaya.
> In the mental attitude seek thy (religious) refuge;
> Wretched are those whose motive is the fruit (of action).
>
> II.49
>
> Except action for the purpose of worship,
> This world is bound by actions;
> Action for that purpose, son of Kuntī,
> Perform thou, free from attachment (to its fruits).
>
> III.9
>
> The disciplined man, abandoning the fruit of actions,
> Attains abiding peace;
> The undisciplined, by action due to desire,
> Attached to the fruit (of action), is bound.
>
> V.12
>
> If thou hast no ability even for practice,
> Be wholly devoted to work for Me;
> For my sake also actions
> Performing, thou shalt win perfection.
>
> But even this thou art unable
> To do, resorting to My discipline,
> Abandonment of the fruit of all actions
> Do thou then effect, controlling thyself.
>
> XII.10-11
>
> However, these actions
> With abandonment of attachment and fruits
> Must be performed: this, son of Pṛthā, is My
> Definite and highest judgment.
>
> XVIII.6

Thus the "final conclusion on the subject is to the effect: 'That rites are not prohibited but that pious works performed without desire are preferable to works performed for the sake of fruition; and he who performs those works without desire, is superior to him who performs works for the sake of fruition". Once this conclusion is drawn, Roy drives home his point:[324]

> If then works without desire are acknowledged by you to be superior to works with desire of fruition, why do you persuade widows to perform work for the sake of fruition, and do not recommend to them rather to follow asceticism, by which they may acquire eternal beatitude ?

But the opponents of the abolition of sati counter with the following objections:

> (1) even if the widow should, on the above argument not commit sati but rather follow an ascetic mode of life, she might fail in the latter course and therefore it is better that she commit sati;
> (2) even the practice of asceticism leads to heavenly rewards, so there is really no difference between the two options of committing sati or leading an ascetic life.

Roy's response is to rebut these arguments by citing specific verses from the *Gītā*. On the first point Roy argues that there is really no such thing as failure on the spiritual path where even a little goes a long way. He cites *Bhagavadgītā* II.40:

> In it there is no loss of a start once made,
> Nor does any reverse occur;
> Even a little of this duty
> Saves from great danger.

This first objection is not hard to rebut. After all, the widow could waver in her resolve to commit sati as well. It is the second objection which is more difficult to counter and Roy's answer to it is accordingly more subtle. He argues in effect that while it is true that both those who perform desire-oriented deeds and those who perform desire-free deeds go to the blessed worlds, the similarity ends there and their fates diverge thereafter. Those whose actions were motivated by desire, after a spell in heaven, enter the world of the mortals and fall in *saṁsāra*. Thus *Bhagavadgītā* IX.21:

> They, after enjoying the expansive world of heaven,
> When their merit is exhausted, enter the world of mortals;
> Thus conforming to the religion of the three (Vedas),
> Men who lust after desires get that which comes and goes.

The Yogī, however, who performs actions without desire, may also be reborn but his upward spiritual mobility remains unimpeded. *Bhagavadgītā* VI.41 is quite explicit on the point:

> Attaining the heavenly worlds of the doers of right,
> Dwelling there for endless years,
> In the house of pure and illustrious folk
> One that has fallen from discipline is born.

This second point turns on the fine distinction between the mere performance of *karma* and the performance of *karma yoga*.

III

The opponent next comes up with a more insidious argument: women are only entitled to the inferior path of action and not of asceticism. And in support of his position the opponent cites from *Bhagavadgītā* III.26:

> Let him not cause confusion of mind
> In ignorant folk who are attached to action;

This may strike the modern reader as an instance of the devil quoting the scripture, but the argument is diabolically clever. The *Gītā* itself seems to warn against confusing people by speaking of desireless action if they think that action without desire is a psychological impossibility.

Roy's refutation[325] comes from the *Gītā* too. He invokes the famous verse which shows the entitlement of women to salvation, the 32nd verse of the IXth chapter:

If they take refuge in Me, son of Pṛthā,
Even those who may be of base origin,
Women, men of the artisan caste, and serfs too,
Even they go to the highest goal.[326]

The opponent had urged that by forsaking sati the widow may lose the fruits of both the lower and the higher paths—heaven and salvation, but the above verse shows that "there is no reason why they should lose both objects of future hope by forsaking concremation".[327]

IV

The opponent of the abolition of sati continues to stick to his guns and produces a fresh argument: that heaven-oriented action is enjoined by the Vedas themselves.[328] Therefore, how could the Vedic injunction be disregarded?

Roy's response is twofold. Firstly, he avails of the criticism in the *Gītā* directed against Vedic ritualism (II.42-44).

This flowery speech which
Undiscerning men utter,
Who take delight in the words of the Veda, son of Pṛthā,
Saying that there is nothing else,

Whose nature is desire, who are intent on heaven,
(The speech) which yields rebirth as the fruit of actions,
Which is replete with various (ritual) acts
Aiming at the goal of enjoyment and power,—

Of men devoted to enjoyment and power,
Who are robbed of insight by that (speech),
A mental attitude resolute in nature
Is not established in concentration.

This is reinforced with a similar passage from the *Bhāgavata Purāṇa.*[329]

Secondly, Roy takes recourse to a more general argument, one with which students of Hinduism are familiar, that, in general, within the Hindu tradition, the school of *uttara-mīmāṁsā* ultimately superseded that of *pūrva-mīmāṁsā*;[330] that the spiritual content of the tradition was finally regarded as transcending the ritual content of the tradition. Roy establishes this point by citing *Bhagavadgītā* X.32c which he translates as "Among Śāstras I am those which treat of God."[331]

V

It is clear, therefore, that Roy not only knew the *Gītā* but used it to forensic effect. The basic argument he used in support of the abolition of sati was the doctrine of desireless action or *niṣkāma karma* as propounded in the *Gītā*, arguing that the goal of heaven sought by the act of sati was an end inferior to that of salvation, to which women were fully entitled, which was to be attained by an ascetic life of desireless activity. Indeed in one passage he asks his opponents rhetorically:[332]

> The *Gītā* is not a rare work, and you are not unacquainted with it. Why then do you constantly mislead women unacquainted with the Sastras, to follow a debased path, by holding out to them as temptations the pleasures of futurity, in defiance of all the Sastras, and merely to please the ignorant?

That the *Bhagavadgītā* should have been made an instrument of social reform is significant in itself; it is also significant in that it set a precedent. For instance, Mahatma Gandhi was later to press *Bhagavadgītā* V:18 into service in his campaign for the abolition of Untouchability.

12

SATI, WIDOWHOOD AND YOGA

This final essay of the collection differs from the rest. The preceding papers have been primarily historical in character but in this paper a phenomenological approach to understanding sati has been adopted. The watchword of phenomenology is "To be the things themselves (*Zu den Sachen*)" and its corollary is the radical suspension (*epoché*) of one's own values in order to describe the phenomenon in its own terms including hidden meanings, the less accessible layers of the phenomenon. As Spiegelberg has said: "...if we want to explore the finer structures of the phenomena for their own sakes, simplicity and economy are instruments that are both blunt and blunting. The genuine will to know calls for the spirit of generosity rather than for that of economy, for reference rather than for subjugation, for the lens rather than for the hammer."[333] Sharpe, writing of the phenomenological method in the study of religion has used equally strong words: it seeks to combine "...complete accuracy of scholarship with complete sympathy of treatment to ensure complete understanding of the religious beliefs and practices of other human beings."[334]

The phenomenological approach has been used to describe many religious phenomena from rituals to beliefs to deities in order to understand such entities on their own terms and ultimately to describe and interpret the religion from within rather than without. It is curious that the method has not been applied to sati, for it is precisely when a religious phenomenon is *phenomenal* and provokes strong emotional reactions that it is most difficult to understand. Such has been the case with sati. Whereas most foreigners who witnessed sati pitied the woman, condemned the act as inhuman, tragic, suicidal or barbaric and rarely admired the woman as heroic or pious,[335] in a former age most Hindus eulogized sati and rarely reviled the practice on ethical grounds. The problem of understanding is made even more complex in that Hindus today also condemn sati. Separated by reform and the passage of time they too are virtually outsiders to the phenomenon with a resulting impasse in sympathetic understanding even though they are fully familiar with the constellation of ideas which contributed to the meaning of sati.

Perhaps a phenomenological study of sati has not been attempted because to try to understand such a practice—which today arouses negative feelings given humanistic values and movements to redress the status of women—could easily place one in a highly invidious position by creating the impression that one is trying to justify the custom. And yet it may be argued that when the task is *understanding*, the full phenomenon must be allowed to come into view even though the custom in the final analysis should continue to be subject to radical critique from a modern perspective and kept safely relegated to the past.

This paper, then, shall attempt to understand what was Hindu about sati, for stripped of the adjective Hindu, sati was nothing but a suicidal act or homicide. Nothing could be further from the traditional Hindu perspective which operated for a number of centuries.[336] To put it simply, the woman who performed sati was viewed as the *ideal Hindu* women. To do justice to the phenomenon qua phenomenon it is important to seek the religious dimension of sati, for only then will it be possible to understand how such a custom could exercise so great a hold over women over so many centuries in different parts of India and that too with an aura of sanctity.

To understand the sati, one must also understand the Hindu widow. Though they represented apparently polar images in that one was auspicious and the other inauspicious, they shared a deep structure and this deep structure will help us to determine how women acted in a Hindu way according to proleptic models passed on by the tradition.

When her husband died a Hindu woman had theoretically two options. She could opt to remain a widow or she could perform sati.[337] The widow was called *vidhavā*, literally, "the one whose husband is gone, i.e. dead".[338] She may be described by the Sanskrit adjective *tapasvinī*,[339] which contains a suitable pun. The word *tapasvinī* is used idiomatically as an exclamation to connote an unfortunate female and can best be rendered

"O poor thing !", whereas *tapasvinī* as a noun signifies the one who practices austerities and in a broad sense is coterminous with *yoginī*, a female *yogī*. The word *satī* means literally a "good woman".[340] The sense of this word, in fact, bestows superlative praise on the woman, as in the expression *satī pārvatī*, the best woman, Pārvatī. The word sati also referred conventionally to the act of *sati*, namely, the self-immolation of a widow on the funeral pyre of her husband. The *vidhavā* was considered to be unfortunate, even inauspicious (*aśubha*). The *satī*, by contrast, was viewed as fortunate and auspicious (*śubha*).[341]

A Hindu may not have identified with the widow's plight unless the widow happened to be a daughter, sister or mother. Even widows themselves cursed, accused, and despised another woman when she lost her husband, thereby joining in public criticism with genuine vigour. The widow was often referred to as a wretched woman with a "shattered fate" which implied that "the pot of her fate" became as empty as her life without her husband and that there was no "substance" to her life. She was as good as dead; and yet, she, the ogress,[342] survived, her god (i.e. her husband) being dead.

The appearance of a traditional widow suggested destitution. It was said that the "lines of misfortune" were written on her "white forehead" because it no longer had the red dot (*tilaka*).[343] Her tonsured head or her flowing hair unadorned with flowers indicated her miserable status. No jewels adorned her nose and ears, no chains her neck, no bangles her wrists, no rings her toes. Clad simply in a cotton sari of prescribed colour, often without blouse she even went about barefoot. Not only was she denied enjoyments, but every other opportunity for pleasure (*bhoga*), such as participation in social gatherings, festivals, the partaking of rich food, indeed, entertainment or pleasure of any sort. So complete was the redefinition of her status and role from wife to widow that she bemoaned the loss of her husband constantly and reflected on her culpability in this regard. She attempted, and was even forced, to justify her deprivation of all fortune. Upon her husband's death she internalized the proleptic model of behaviour for a widow. The family and society imposed on her the proper image and behaviour through their reactions to her as they deprived her of *bhoga*, social privileges, religious rites, and economic well being.[344] Even when they grieved ostensibly for her plight they had more regret for her Karmic crime of "causing her husband's death". Thus widowhood of a woman entailed spiritual misfortune and implied the temporary absence of *dharma*[345] in relation to the family. Not only she but also the family, the lineage and the community too had to share the blame for this *adharma*.[346]

Whereas most Hindus looked down on the *vidhavā*, they had a diametrically opposite attitude towards the sati.[347] The self-cremation of the sati was one of the most fortunate and auspicious events for the sati herself and for those who witnessed this rare expression of spirituality. It was as though sati were an event of spiritual and cosmic significance. For the woman who opted for sati, sati was like the performance of a religious ceremony.[348] To capture its religious significance we shall describe the "ideal" event, which inspired the individual acts of sati.

The woman's decision was to be a formal vow (*saṁkalpa*), immediate and without deliberation.[349] She herself was to order calmly the preliminaries of the *sati* rite and in some regions she was to don her bridal sari. Though others were to implore her to reconsider her decision, especially for the sake of her children, she was not to listen to them. She was to bless them benevolently.[350] She was not to shed a tear, even though great lamentation surrounded her, for she was to look upon this moment as the most auspicious of her life. This was to be the supreme opportunity for self-sacrifice that consummated her life of dedication to her husband. As if departing on a joyous journey, she was to prostrate herself before the elders and to ask for their blessings. They were to bless her generously and, reversing the usual norms of respect, were to prostrate to her in return. Indeed they were to look upon her as the goddess incarnate. As she led the procession to the cremation ground where the corpse of her husband was awaiting cremation, she was to be joined by the people of the village who came to witness this awesome event.[351] After the performance of the preliminary rites, she was to bid final farewell with folded hands (*praṇāmāñjali*). With perfect tranquillity, she was to climb the ladder, sit down on the pyre and tenderly take her husband's head on her lap. Optionally she was to recline beside him. Even when the flames reached her, she was to maintain her composure.

The crowd was to acclaim her as a "good wife", a true sati, one who had brought immense dignity and honour to herself, her family, and her community. Not only were they to say that she had conferred the sacrality of the tradition (*paramparā*) on her family, but they also were to express gratitude that they themselves had had a chance to witness this noble sacrifice.[352] This is the ideal sati, the woman and her act.

A Hindu woman was brought up to be a good woman, a sati in the literal sense of the word. As a responsible member of Hindu society she was to conform to the protocols of Hindu *dharma*. What was her special *dharma* as a woman (*strī-dharma*)? The orientation of a traditional Hindu woman may be characterized as union with the husband. As a maiden, the Hindu female was brought up to direct her attention towards securing a husband, whose image, though abstract, received her unswerving devotion. Whether she was given away in marriage as a child or as an adult, a Hindu girl was educated to be a good wife, that is, to be good to her husband. This "goodness' to the husband was central to the definition of *strī-dharma*. This religious psychology was inculcated in maidenhood through various means such as religious instruction, imposition of vows (*vratas*)—fasting being the essential factor—constant instruction by the mother in order to generate and cultivate the virtues of devotion and self-sacrifice, and finally repeated reminders that pleasing the husband, the god (*patideva*), was the whole and sole goal of woman's life. This insistence had the desired effect. For a Hindu woman, the husband became the *sine qua non* of her existence. She believed that her single-pointed concentration and acts of austerity performed for her husband (*pati*) procured good merit (*puṇya*), which would ensure her husband's longevity and prosperity. Due to this orientation she felt that she was responsible if her husband died before her. She thought that she was lacking in her dharmic quality, her goodness, i.e. her *satītva*, if her husband was deprived of life. Consequently, irrespective of his age and the circumstances of his death, she interpreted the event as indicative of her own karmic failure. Shock, grief and guilt therefore characterized her response to his death. With her god departed she truly became *vidhavā*, without fortune. Her immediate act was to undergo religious expiation, whether voluntary or socially imposed, so that she ensured her reunion with her husband in her next birth, or for seven lives to come.

Thus to become *satī* again, a good woman, she was expected to become like a *tapasvinī*, an ascetic woman. She was to practise austerities (*tapas*), which would purify her. It was as though she were undertaking a *sādhanā*, a yogic discipline. Her *tapas* was fourfold in function: 1. redemptive, 2. meritorious, 3. stoic and 4. beneficent—in order to regenerate her *satītva*, womanly goodness. Her *tapas* was redemptive in that it expiated the bad *karma* which caused her husband's untimely death. Her *tapas* was meritorious in that it created good *karma* for the next life in order to prevent the recurrence of such a misfortune. Her *tapas* led to stoicism in that it developed endurance and indifference in her through which she became spiritually strong and impervious to mundane desires and pressures. Finally, her *tapas* was beneficient in that it consisted of her serenity, purity, and selflessness which radiated spirituality. From this fourfold function of *tapas* the widow emerged like a *yoginī* with single-pointed concentration, in this case on her husband and on her discipline directed toward reunion with him in his next birth. She utilized the hiatus of time from her husband's death to her own in order to retrieve the auspicious state of marriage and her *satītva*.

This gradual recovery of *satītva* was the goal of a Hindu widow. She accepted it, even though she may not have understood the theory underlying it. The society imposed it on her. Both her understanding and the society's knowledge of what her course of widowhood ought to be were in tune with each other. It may be argued that her discipline is best understood as akin to the discipline of *yoga* and her goal as similar to the goal of *yoga* (in that she too desired union, albeit in this case union with the husband).

But, can the discipline of a widow be compared legitimately to *yoga*, and, if so, what kind of *yoga*? According to Patañjali's *Yoga-sūtras*[353] the definition of *yoga* as a discipline is the "restraint of mental activities." Its corollary is the concentration on a single point (*ekāgratā*), for *ekāgratā* results in insensitivity to all distracting stimuli. *Ekāgratā* is fostered by disciplines that involve restraints (*yama*) and ascetic practices (*niyama*). *Yama*, for example, involves such restraints as sexual continence (*brahmacarya*) and non-possession (*aparigraha*), which purify the aspirant. *Niyama* includes mental discipline to eliminate desire and transcend the tensions created by pairs of opposites (*dvandvas*). Hence the *yogī* gradually overcomes all temptations and doubts. This enables him to focus increasingly on God with single-pointed concentration and to fortify his yogic power by overcoming all obstacles. He emerges impervious to his environment and to his own past.

When the description of a widow is compared to that of a *yogī*, we notice certain parallels.[354] A widow's *ekāgratā* was her unswerving devotion to her departed husband. She too practised *brahmacarya*, perfect sexual abstinence in speech, mind, and act. She possessed little. That was her *aparigraha*. She became serene as she eradicated all desires and went beyond such polarities (*dvandvas*) as comfort and discomfort, pleasure and sorrow, honour and dishonour. Just as the *yogī* overcomes temptations by renouncing house-holdership (*gṛhasthāśrama*), the widow renounced the bonds of family. She too overcame obstacles, in her case indifference, curse, and rejection from society, and thereby fortified her yogic power. Like a *yogī*, the widow became impervious to society, in her case through maltreatment and the accusation of being an ogress.

To characterize such a *yoga* exercised by the widow we coin the term *patiyoga*.[355] The word *patiyoga* may be interpreted in two ways: 1. *yoga* as the means (*upāya*) for passing through the stage of widowhood in preparation for reunion with the husband and 2. *yoga* as the goal (*upeya*), which is reunion with the husband in the next birth. Though according to the popular view a true *yogī* is one whose goal is *mokṣa* (release from the cycles of existence) and *yogīs* were almost always men, a widow may be viewed as a *yoginī*, since her *upāya* and *upeya* paralleled his. There is, however, one significant difference: a woman generally overlooked the ultimacy of *mokṣa* and concentrated instead on reunion with her husband as her ultimate goal. With her spiritual intent to reunite with her husband for the next seven lives she was rebirth-oriented[356] in contradistinction to the *yogī's mokṣa*-orientation.

Now we are in a position to assert that underlying the surface image of the widow as a deprived person is the image of the widow as a *yoginī*. These two images of the widow are not antithetical but structurally similar.

It seems to us that widowhood was viewed as the inauspicious hiatus between two states of auspicious union.

Present life		*Future life*
auspicious	inauspicious	auspicious
(union/marriage)	(widowhood)	reunion

The widow gradually overcame the opposition between the auspiciousness of married life and the inauspiciousness of widowhood through the fourfold *tapas* and lived like a *yoginī*. Her own death heralded reunion with her husband. While the death of her husband was viewed as inauspicious, her own death was not thought to be so since it signalled auspicious reunion with him. Thus the hiatus of widowhood was not a meaningless vacuum. It was temporally given and karmically productive. Accordingly a Hindu widow utilized the intervening period to excel in patiyogic *sādhanā* (discipline).

Comparing the images of the widow and the sati, we note certain parallels. Just as the widow was anxious to reunite with her husband, so was the satī. Just as the widow developed perfect discipline (*yoga*) in her austerities, so too the sati exercised yogic control in her act of sati. Just as the widow performed the fourfold *tapas* so did the sati. The sati burned away all defilements by entering the conflagration; she became purified and produced good *karma* for the next life; her instantaneous resolve to undergo sati indicated her fortitude, which she had cultivated through her training; and she too radiated benevolence.

From the accounts, however, sati and widowhood did not constitute equal options. From the moment of her decision the sati was considered auspicious. The widow from the moment of her husband's death became inauspicious; in fact, even her gradual metamorphosis to a *yoginī*-like figure failed to generate public veneration for her, though her saint-like behaviour earned her respect despite the label ogress. The sati's resolve, on the contrary, eliminated completely the accusation that she was an ogress. The sati never had the title of widow. Because of the immediacy of her self-imposed death she circumvented any rite of passage to another stage of life.[357] Rather, she donned her wedding garments and thereby reaffirmed symbolically her marital status and auspiciousness. Everyone in the village gathered to witness the sati's holiness, whereas everyone avoided the sight of the widow. While all gathered to hear the sati's benedictions, they shut their ears to the widow's utterance.

Still one might ask why the sati was esteemed highly and the widow dishonoured while both of them subjected themselves to different kinds of extreme ordeals? The sati was viewed as a perfect wife, the very embodiment of the goddess,[358] for she expedited *immediately* her bad karma that caused the husband's death. The widow took time to rectify her faults and perfect her yogic discipline to join her husband. Thus the goal (*upeya*) was the same for both, but the means (*upāya*) differed.

Another striking difference between the widow and the sati is witnessed in certain beliefs regarding the death and rebirth of the husband. It was believed that the Hindu Vedic funeral ritual (*antyeṣṭi*) offered a promise of heaven after death. The fulfilment of the promise was, however, conditional upon one's *karma*. If a surplus of demerit was suspected, the *antyeṣṭi* was believed to be ritually ineffective as "insurance" for the attainment of heaven. But there was a way around this problem. At the sign of the impending death of a man, the family physician warned the family to prepare for the ritual proceedings to ensure the dying man's afterlife in heaven. Pilgrimage to sacred places (*tīrthayātrā*) was recommended as one of the efficacious means to accomplish this since death at a holy place was thought to guarantee heaven. If the plan of pilgrimage could not be implemented and the husband died, then a "good wife" would consider the course of sati to be obligatory on her part to save her husband from the possible deprivation of heaven after death.

One can readily see why the sati was respected more than the widow though both were faced with similar ordeals. Moreover, the sati generated through her self-sacrifice so much merit that not only her husband but she too attained heaven after death.[359]

Irrespective of the merit of this logic, it indeed intimidated and shamed the widow who survived her husband with the lingering doubt as to whether her husband was going to be in heaven on his own merit or in hell or reborn on earth. She worried that in case he was in heaven, whether she would have sufficient merit (*puṇya*) to be eligible for entrance to heaven to be with him there. If he was in hell, she worried whether she should await the exhaustion of his demerit or acquire more merit through her austerities so that she could rescue him by the force of her merit. If, however, he was to be reborn on earth, how was she to avoid the possibility of missing him? The widow's survival after her husband's death was fraught with such doubts as to where he was, how she could rejoin him and how she could redress any negative situation.[360] The sati, on the other hand, had the guarantee not only of reunion with her husband but precisely heaven as their meeting place. The widow, however, was insecure, not only in this life but with regard to her future after death.

Let us now strengthen our claim to the sati's superior status by comparing her triumphant end to that of a *yogī*. Just as the sati ordered preparations for her Great Departure, so the *yogī* who volunteered his mortal extinction also requested the preliminaries for his Great Departure by entering fire, drowning at a *tīrtha* (pilgrimage place), burying himself alive (*samādhi*) or walking and fasting until dead (*mahāprasthāna*). Both of them felt that mortal existence had nothing to offer to them any more, though their reasons for this feeling differed. And for both of them union was central to their orientations. Hence, the *yogī* was the ideal man, the sati the ideal woman.

Our purpose in this paper was to restore the religious dimension to the description and interpretation of the proleptic models of the Hindu widow and sati. The religious categories of *strīdharma*, auspiciousness (*śubha*), and inauspiciousness (*aśubha*) were central to this enterprise, for they were used by the tradition itself. An analysis of the deep structure of the proleptic models of the Hindu widow and sati, however, revealed a *hidden* religious dimension: yoga.

We are aware that the Hindu widow and sati themselves were not conscious of the yogic dimension of their life. They would not have technically identified themselves as *yoginī*. Their domestic ideals and rebirth orientation precluded their appropriation of the concept of *yoga* in its technical, conventional sense of the religious discipline for, and goal of, liberation (*mokṣa*). However, by using the term *yoga* in its generalized sense, we detected that the psychology of *yoga* was indeed instilled, albeit inadvertently, in the traditional Hindu woman. This was evident in the concept of *tapasvinī*, the word that describes literally and figuratively the Hindu widow just as the word *tapasvī* describes the *yogī*. That a sati could be buried alive rather than be burned by fire, just as the *yogī* could undergo self-immolation rather than bury himself alive, strengthens the claim that both the sati and the *yogī* share a similar deep structure.[361] It is tempting to suggest that *bhaktiyoga*, the yoga of devotion to God mediated the male and female orientations and in some sects ultimately fused them in the sense that devotion to the *pati* (God husband) had as its corollary the attainment of Supreme Heaven and salvation itself.[362]

Following the phenomenological method we bracketed our modern and humanistic values to allow the phenomenon to appear fully. Our task of understanding the traditional Hindu proleptic models of the widow and sati completed, we may remove the bracket to evaluate the phenomenon once more. From a critical perspective we find that the male *yogī* and the female *yoginī* as sati and *vidhavā* are different in ways not apparent in the above discussion. A man has real freedom of choice. He may opt to become a *yogī*. Even if his family tries to discourage him, he transcends their constraints and criticisms, for the religion and the society view the yogic path as a way to attain liberation, the *summum bonum* of existence. Even if a man opts to become a householder, he may live so respectably and if his wife should die before him, he may opt to marry again. At any time during marriage he may opt to become a *yogī*. A woman, on the other hand, according to the normative view, had to be married if she was to be respectable in society. If her husband died first, she ostensibly had an option: but even this occurred within the theoretical framework of marriage: she was to be reunited with her husband. Her only option was how to do this: immediately by sati or slowly by living out her life as a widow. Furthermore, in the case of the sati, her option to join her husband through self-immolation was supposed to be her own, though it can be argued that the proleptic model instilled in her from childhood was the society's or family's choice not truly hers. Given the hard life of a widow and the ostensible lack of respect, sati may have seemed the best of the two options, an escape from hardship. In some cases, then, sati was more involuntary than voluntary although the satī's resolve (*saṁkalpa*) was to be her own and any force used after the formal declaration was viewed as help to hold her to her intention, rather than forcing her to perform sati. Even the latter point from a modern standpoint is cause for concern, for it does not allow the woman to change her mind when it is her own life which is at stake.

As for the widow, her only option was sati, which may have held the promise of heaven and veneration of her name on earth but took supreme courage. Moreover, the imposition of the proleptic model of widowhood on a woman may have been considered dharmic but may, in fact, have constituted cruelty on the part of the woman's family and society, who wished her dead rather than inauspiciously alive. That a widow did not understand the deep religious structures that molded her life and could not positively appropriate the dimension of *yoga* also seems today to be a great injustice, especially when the *yogī's tapas* is esteemed and here appeared as deprivation caused by her bad *karma*.

Now we have two understandings of the proleptic model of the Hindu widow and the sati. The first is situated in the organic milieu of traditional Hinduism, the second is situated in a modern perspective informed by history, psychology, sociology and feminism. It is difficult to sustain these two perspectives simultaneously but perhaps a stereoscopic vision from the traditional and modern "lenses" will energe and help us comprehend why the meaning of the models of the Hindu widow and sati is more complex than may be immediately apparent.[363]

NOTES

1. Quoted by G.T. Garratt, *An Indian Commentary* (London: Jonathan Cape, year ?), p. 235.

2. William Ward, *Necessity of Christianity to India* (Boston: January 1, 1821), p. 2. Also see note 59.

3. Monier Williams, *Indian Wisdom* (London: H. Allen and Co., 1875), p. 258, fn. 2. Sometimes it involved co-interment, and rarely co-immersion, vide Edward Thompson, *Suttee* (London: George Allen and Unwin, 1928), p. 39.

4. William Crooke, ed., *Sir H. Yule and A.C. Burnell's Hobson-Jobson* (Delhi: Munshiram Manoharlal, 1968), Article on "Suttee", p. 878.

5. There might be some room for difference of opinion on whether sati should be called a *rite* or a *custom*. For if the notion of rite involves that of a religious ceremony, Horace Wilson was among the earlier scholars to show that *satis* are not "essentially a part of the Hindu religion". But then, as Lord William Bentinck remarked in the minute of November 8, 1829: "I entirely agree in this opinion. The question is not what the rite is but what it is supposed to be, and I have no doubt that the conscientious belief of every order of Hindus, with few exceptions, regard it as sacred", vide Ramsey Muir, *The Making of British India*, 1756-1858 (Manchester: University Press, 1915), p. 294. For a possible mode of transformation from custom to rite see N.M. Penzer, ed., *The Ocean of Story*, Vol. IV (London: Chas. J. Sawyer, 1925), p. 262. The distinction between custom and rite, however, has not played any key role in the sati issue and hence sati will be referred to as either.

6. Sometimes, especially with kings, officers, servants and horses etc. were also cremated along with wives, vide N.M. Penzer, *op. cit.*, pp. 256, 270 etc. The term sati, however, should refer only to the concremation of wives and concubines though in the last legal case of sati in Udaipur in 1861, when all the legal wives of the Maharaja refused, "a slave girl was induced to become a Sati" (A.S. Altekar, *The Position of Women in Hindu Civilization* [Delhi: Motilal Banarsidass, 1962] p. 142).

7. Sometimes she burnt herself after her husband's cremation, vide Edward Thompson, *op. cit.*, p. 15. There is a scandalous case of a widow who was "goaded by her family into the expression of a wish to burn with some relic of her husband, twelve months after her husband's death" in Banaras in 1806. She jumped from the pile into the river and was rescued by a police boat. A tense situation developed which was brought under control by Charles Harding, the magistrate, vide Philip Woodruff, *The Men Who Ruled India*, Vol. I (London: Jonathan Cape, 1953) p. 256.

8. See Vincent A. Smith, *The Oxford History of India* (Oxford: Clarendon Press, 1919) p. 644, fn. 1. Edward Thompson tried to distinguish between the two usages by using SATI for the person and SUTTEE for the rite, vide Edward Thompson, *op. cit.*, pp. 15-16, but the attempt does not seem to have succeeded.

Most dictionaries use the two forms interchangeably, e.g., *New Standard Dictionary of the English Language* (New York: Funk and Wagnalls Co. 1951), p. 2178.

9. *Encyclopedia Britannica*, Vol. 21 (London: William Benton, 1969), p. 466. N.M. Penzer (*op. cit.*, p. 258), also Edward Thompson (*op. cit.*, p. 15, etc.), remarks on this that the "Sanskrit word *satī* is a feminine noun meaning "good", "devout", "true" and consequently it denotes a person and not a practice. The application of the substantive to the act instead of to the person is European." However, the form to commit sati or to become sati has an Indian parallel. A popular Hindi couplet takes a fling at womanly wantonness thus:

Tiyā carit jāne nā koī,
Patī mār ke sattī hoī.

This may be paraphrased as: female character is inscrutable. She is capable of "becoming a Sati" after killing her own husband. This writer has not been able to date the saying: if it is pre-18th century, then the expression "becoming Suttee" would seem to have roots in Indian use; if not, this might be a feedback into Hindi of the English usage. Bengali, however, does not use the word Sati in the sense of rite.

It may also be noted that although in popular usage the word sati is used for immolation with the husband, in the mythology of Hinduism though Pārvatī, qua Satī "destroyed herself by fire; but in this case, though she proved herself a faithful wife, she did not burn herself with her husband's body", W.J. Wilkins, *Modern Hinduism* (London: T. Fisher Unwin, 1887), p. 377.

10. The use of an Anglicised expression, Suttee, to denote a Hindu rite itself serves to illustrate a linguistic feature of the Indo-Western encounter. This feature has two aspects: one, the popular use of Western or Anglicised Indian terms to describe Hindu rites and customs and two, the often incorrect use of these terms. This has led to academically unfortunate consequences. For instance, the use of the word Caste System-a Portuguese legacy-obscured for decades the distinction between Varṇa and Jāti, vide M.N. Srinivas, *Caste in Modern India* (New Delhi: Asia Publishing House, 1962), and *Religion and Society Among the Coorgs of South India* (Oxford University Press, 1952), passim; K.M. Panikkar, *Hindu Society at the Cross Roads* (Bombay: Asia Publishing House, 1955), p. 10; Irawati Karve, *Hindu Society—An Interpretation* (Poona: Deccan College, 1961), p. 11, etc. As will be pointed out later, sati, in Hindu usage, was known as SAHAMARAṆA when the widow underwent immolation along with her dead husband and ANUMARAṆA when the immolation occurred after the husband's cremation. The expressions SAHAGAMANA and ANUGAMANA were also sometimes used, vide Edward Thompson, *op. cit.*, p. 15. JAUHAR occurred when the wife or wives immolated themselves, often communally, in anticipation of the husband's expected death, vide *Encyclopedia Britannica*, Vol. 21, *op. cit.*, p. 466. Moreover, in Hindu usage the word SATĪ means "a good woman", "a faithful wife" and also refers to the mythological figure of that name, the wife of Śiva who immolated herself to avenge her husband's insult at the hands of her father, vide R.J. Blackham, *Incomparable India* (London: Sampson Low, 1935) pp. 37-38. Sati is also a goddess, vide M.W.

Pinkham, *Woman in the Sacred Scriptures of Hinduism* (New York: Columbia University Press, 1941), p. 93.

11. The earliest historical record of sati is found in Greek sources, vide A.S. Altekar, *op. cit.*, p. 122, etc. The earliest scriptural record is found in the Mahābhārata vide *Encyclopedia Britannica*, Vol. 21, *op. cit.*, p. 466; A.S. Altekar, *op. cit.*, p. 120, etc. The earliest epigraphic record is found in the 6th century A.D., vide Louis Renou, *The Nature of Hinduism* (New York: Walker and Company, 1964), p. 83.

12. The source is the Greek author Diodorus Siculus, who flourished in the 1st century B.C. but his account pertains to the Punjab of 4th century B.C., vide *Encyclopedia Britannica*. Vol. 21, *op. cit.*, p. 466. Another source is Onesicritus, vide N.M. Penzer, *op. cit.*, p. 261.

13. The husband being, of course, John F. Kennedy, 35th President of the United States of America.

14. The two dates correspond to two major landmarks in the British period of Indian history: namely, the Battle of Plassey (1757) which laid the foundation of British Raj and the so-called Mutiny (1857) which shook it. The third landmark is, of course, the liquidation of British Raj in 1947.
The last legal case of sati occurred in 1861 A.D. Hence one could revise the terminal year for the second period—the 1757-1857 period. This writer has chosen to abide by the historically established divide.
For the chronology see R.C. Majumdar, H.C. Raychaudhuri and Kalikinkar Datta, *An Advanced History of India* (New York: St Martin's Press, 1967), pp. 1063-1071. Also note that the battle against sati "was indeed won by 1850 and the Suttee in 1861 was merely its last shot", Sir Percival Griffiths, *The British Impact on India* (London: Cass, 1965), p. 225.

15. Keteus-Ketu or Khatri? speculates Monier-Williams, *op. cit.*, p. 258.

16. A.S. Altekar, *op. cit.*, p. 122; see N.M. Penzer, *op. cit.*, p. 261.

17. For a description of this sati, see N.M. Penzer, *op. cit.*, p. 261; for actual quotation translated from Greek see R.C. Majumdar, ed., *The Age of Imperial Unity* (Bombay: Bharatiya Vidya Bhavan, 1953), pp. 567-8.

18. N.M. Penzer, *op. cit.*, p. 262.

19. See Edward Thompson, *op. cit.*, p. 44.

20. *Ibid.*, p. 28. See William Crooke, ed., *op. cit.*, pp. 879-881.

21. R.C. Majumdar, H.C. Raychaudhuri, K. Datta, *op. cit.*, p. 623.

22. N.M. Penzer, *op. cit.*, p. 263. The Commentary says: "If any Hindu died his wife was to burn herself of her own free will, and when she was proceeding to this self-sacrifice it was with great merrymaking and blowing of music, saying that she desired to accompany her husband to the other world...However, when Alfonso de Albuquerque took the city of Goa he forbade them that time forth that any more women should be burned, and though to change one's custom is equal to death itself, nevertheless they were happy to save their lives, and spake very highly of him because he had ordered that there should be no more burning". Quoted by R.W. Frazer, *British India* (New York: G.P. Putnam's Sons, 1918), pp. 207-8.
Please see next footnote where this is contradicted. The point, then, arises: was Portuguese abolition of sati welcomed as the Commentary would have us

believe, or did it arouse misgivings as some British writers seem to think? Was it a case of mixed reactions here too, some being pleased and others aggrieved as with the abolition of sati in British India? In the British case, we are told, "It is difficult to form an accurate estimate of public opinion on the abolition of the 'Sati'", R.C. Majumdar, ed., *Britisn Paramountcy and Indian Renaissance*, Part II (Bombay: Bharatiya Vidya Bhavan, 1965,) p. 293, fn. 20.

23. It is of some interest to note that the subsequent British reluctance to abolish sati had something to do with the Portuguese experience, whose unpopularity the British were in no mood to emulate. This unpopularity was partly attributed to their proclivity to interfere with native customs especially on Christian grounds; see Philip Woodruff, *The Men Who Ruled India, op. cit.*, Vol. I, p. 242.

24. N.M. Penzer *op. cit.*, p. 270.

25. P.J. Marshall, ed., *The British Discovery of Hinduism in the Eighteenth Century* (Cambridge: University Press, 1970), p. 97.

26. John Zephaniah Holwell however, doubts the veracity of this; vide P.J. Marshall, *ibid.*, p. 97. Cinematic echoes of the account are perhaps found in "Around the World in Eighty Days".

27. *Ibid.*

28. Sometimes the only possible reaction seems to be one of amazement as Nicolo Conti, the 15th century Italian visitor, presumably felt when he learnt that the Raja of Vijayanagar had 12,000 wives of whom 2,000 or 3,000 were selected "*on condition* that at his death they should *voluntarily* burn themselves", vide Robert Sewell, *A Forgotten Empire* (London: Swan Sonnenschein, 1900), p. 84, emphasis added.

29. William Johns, *A Collection of Facts and Opinions Relative to the Burning of Widows with the Dead Bodies of their Husbands* (Birmingham: W.H. Pearce, 1816), pp. 7-8.

30. R.C. Zaehner, *Hinduism* (London: Oxford University Press, 1962), p. 147.

31. A.S. Altekar, *op. cit.*, p. 136.

32. William Johns, *op. cit.*, p. 2.

33. *Ibid.*, p. 15. But even Bernier's accounts at places are not without elements of admiration; see A.S. Altekar, *op. cit.*, p. 136.

34. William Johns, *op. cit.*, p. 13.

35. R.C. Majumdar, ed., *op. cit.*, pp. 54, 60.

36. P.E. Roberts, *History of British India* (Oxford: Clarendon Press, 1923), Chp. V-VIII.

37. A.S. Altekar, *op. cit.*, pp. 122-3.

38. *Ibid.*, p. 137.

39. *Ibid.*, p. 135.

40. *Ibid.*, p. 139. To make the widow commit sati was one way of reducing claims on property.

41. Percival Spear, *India* (Ann Arbor: University of Michigan Press, 1961), p. 144.

42. *Ibid.*, Chp. XV.

43. *Ibid.*, Chp. XVII-XXII.

44. R.C. Majumdar et al., *op. cit.*, p. 661.

45. P.E. Roberts, *op. cit.*, pp. 158-60.

46. A mention of sati by a 16th century British trader, Ralph Fitch, is perhaps appropriately matter-of-fact. "Wives here doe burne with their husbands when they die, if they will not their heads be shaven and never any account of them is made afterward", vide R.W. Frazer, *op. cit.*, pp. 23-24.

47. *Encyclopedia Britannica*, Vol. 15, op. cit., p. 577.

48. *Ibid.*, p. 578.

49. Percival Spear, *op. cit.*, p. 290.

50. Dr Carey in March 1799, Mr Ward on March 2, 1802 and Mr Marshman on August 13, 1803, vide William Johns, *op. cit.*, pp. 23-26.

51. See George Smith, *The Life of William Carey* (London: John Murray, 1885), p. 279. For Christian attitude to sati see B.N. Pandey, *The Break-up of the British Empire* (New York: St. Martin's Press, 1969), p. 28; R.C. Majumdar, ed., *op. cit.*, Part II, p. 271; for Christian missionary account, see Abbe J.A. Dubois, *Hindu Manners, Customs and Ceremonies* (Oxford: Clarendon Press, 1959), Chp. XIX.

52. William Johns, *op. cit.*, p. vi. It is initially a bit puzzling that the name of James Mill does not figure in the sati controversy. After all he is the author of the voluminous *The History of British India* (New York: Chelsea House Publishers, 1968) which was written around that time. Moreover, it contains a well-known phillipic against Hinduism (Book II). Why then his curious reticence to make a fiery issue out of sati? Though he observes: "Of the modes adopted by Hindus of sacrificing themselves to divine powers, none, however, has more excited the attention of Europeans than the burning of wives on the funeral piles of their husbands" (James Mill, *op. cit.*, p. 289), yet he, on his own, does not lambaste sati. The reason seems to lie in James Mill's heavy reliance on Manu (see Note A to volumes I and II). Manu explicitly mentions that women are to be cared for in old age by sons; vide Mahamahopadhyaya Ganganath Jha, *Manu Smṛti* (University of Calcutta, 1926), p. 3, and is silent on sati. Moreover, Mill never witnessed a sati.

53. Edward Thompson, *op. cit.*, p. 69. According to more sensational writings, in the whole of India, "not less than five thousand of these unfortunate women, it is supposed, are immolated every twelve months", vide Rev. William Ward, *A View of the History, Literature and Religion of the Hindus* (Hartford: H. Huntington, 1824), p. 57.

54. Sophia Dobson Collet, *The Life and Letters of Raja Rammohun Roy* (Calcutta: Sadharan Brahmo Samaj, 1962), p. 82.

55. Edward Thompson, *op. cit.*, p. 69. No one quite knows why sati seems to increase after the establishment of British Raj in Bengal. Three explanations have been offered: (1) that "this increase is apparent rather than real; that the cases were more carefully reported, and not that more actually occurred", W.J. Wilkins, *Modern Hinduism* (London: T. Fisher Unwin, 1887), p. 390; (2) that it is due to epidemics, vide E. Thompson, *op. cit.*, p. 73; (3) that British tolerance of sati was mistaken for approval (see note 93).

56. Sophia Dobson Collet, *op. cit.*, p. 76.

57. Edward Thompson, *op. cit.*, p. 69.

58. Sophia Dobson Collet, *op. cit.*, p. 90.

59. *Ibid.*, p. 194. It is, perhaps, of some interest that in 1821 the polemics on sati also reached the shores of America. In fact, it reached Boston. On January 1, 1821 a tract entitled "Necessity of Christianity to India" was distributed here. The authorship is not specified but the tract mentions all the three members of the Serampore trio: Mr Marshman (p. 1), Mr Ward (p. 2) and Dr Carey (p. 3). It mentions Mr Ward as one who "has brought with him from India an official document, signed by the British magistrates, from which it appears that in one of the three Presidencies of British India only, the Presidency of Bengal, in the year 1817, *Seven hundred and six widows* were BURNT ALIVE or BURIED ALIVE" and then follows an inflammatory account of the rite of sati with a call to save 150,000 beings from the fire of Hinduism, so to say, by bringing to them the "light of Christianity". Ten years later, in 1831, there was distributed in Providence "A Reply to the little tract entitled 'Necessity of Christianity in India' distributed in this vicinity by William Ward, an Indian missionary". This Reply called upon the "cruel churchmen before thou art liberal to extenuate the anguish of the funeral pile" to "sheath thy sword already whetted to goad the bowels of thy French, British or Indian brother". The call was to "scatter to the wind thy murderous powder, and beat thy war-provoking musket and deadly bayonet, into instruments of innocent husbandry before thou pitieth the Hindu widow" (p. 8 of D.B. Slack's *A Reply to...*).

60. *Essays Relative to the Habits, Character and Moral Improvement of the Hindoos* (London: Kingsbury, Parbury and Allen, 1823), pp. 1-86.

61. P.E. Roberts, *op. cit.*, p. 303; E. Thompson, *op. cit.*, pp. 70-71.

62. E. Thompson, *op. cit.*, p. 73.

63. J. Pegg, *The Suttee's Cry to Britain* (London: Seely and Son, 1827).

64. See Sophia Dobson Collet, *op. cit.*, Chp. VII, especially pp. 254-258.

65. This Regulation had been promulgated the previous day, Dec. 4, 1829; vide Sophia Dobson Collet, *op. cit.*, p. 259.

66. F. Deaville Walker, *William Carey* (Chicago: Moody Press, 1951), p. 252.

67. See E. Thompson, *op. cit.*, pp. 78-81.

68. For an unusually graphic account of this, see Edward Thompson, *op. cit.*, Chp. VIII.

69. Cases of illegal sati continued to occur, vide E. Thompson, *op. cit.*, Chp. IX. Peter Muir, writing in 1943, mentions the "last known incident" as of 1932, vide his *This is India* (New York: Doubleday, Doran and Co., 1943), p. 34. For a case as late as 1946, see A.S. Altekar, *op. cit.*, p. 137.

70. There is, however, a remarkable exception in John Zephaniah Holwell. It is remarkable because amidst a near-unanimous chorus of condemnation he speaks with a different voice and tries to present a justification for sati. He admits that "our fair countrywomen shudder at an action" like sati which he fears "they will look upon as proof of the highest infatuation of their sex". Though it is not his "intention here to defend the tenets of the Brahmins" he wishes to "be allowed to offer some justification on behalf of the Gentoo women". In trying to "view it (as we should every other action) without prejudice and without keeping always in sight our own tenets and customs", he comes to the conclusion that Hindu women, in committing sati "act upon heroic, as well as

rational and pious principles" (sic.); vide P.J. Marshall, *op. cit.*, pp. 95-96. What makes these remarks even more remarkable is that they should be made by Holwell to whose "fertile imagination" must be ascribed "the tragic details" of the Black Hole. (See R.C. Majumdar et al., *op. cit.*, p. 650). Thus Holwell was a sensationalist and an imperialist so far as Black Hole goes (see Percival Spear, *op. cit.*, p. 202), but his stance on sati is curiously different. We find the same thing with James Mill and Vincent Smith, well known imperialist historians, yet not using the abolition of sati as an important justification of British Raj.

71. The nature of the "Mutiny" has been a source of extended and prolonged controversy, and it is not yet clear whether the so-called "Mutiny" was just a Mutiny or something more; vide R.C. Majumdar et al., *op. cit.*, p. 774.

72. Monier Williams, *op. cit.*, p. 259, fn.

73. Sophia Dobson Collet, *op. cit.*, p. 257. His warning was that any public enactment might give rise to general apprehension on the following reasoning: "While the English were contending for power they deemed it politic to allow universal toleration and to respect our religion, but having obtained the supremacy their first act is a violation of the profession, and the next will probably be, like the Muhammadan Conqueror, to force upon us their own religion". H.H. Wilson was also opposed to the abolition of sati by legal fiat; vide R.C. Majumdar, ed., *Britisn Paramountcy and Indian* Renaissance, *op. cit.*, Part II, p. 274.

74. For the role of the abolition of sati as a causal factor in the "Mutiny" see Surendra Nath Sen, *Eighteen Fifty Seven* (New Delhi: Govt of India Publication Division, 1957); R.C. Majumdar, ed., *British Paramountcy and Indian Renaissance*, Vol. I (Bombay: Bharatiya Vidya Bhavan, 1963), p, 422; Amaury de Riencourt, *The Soul of India* (New York: Harper Brothers, 1960) p. 207; J.C. Powell Price, *A History of India* (New York: Thomas Nelson and Sons Ltd., 1955), p. 547, etc.

75. An incident from Raja Rammohun Roy's life seems to illustrate this. Lord William Bentinck wished to consult Raja Rammohun Roy on the issue of sati but the Raja sent back the aide-de-camp with the reply that, "I am withdrawn from worldly affairs and am devoted to the reading of the Sastras", etc. Thereupon Lord William Bentinck sent the aide-de-camp with instructions that this time he should not say, "Lord William Bentinck will be pleased to see you", but that "Mr William Bentinck will be highly obliged if you will kindly see him once", vide Sophia Dobson Collect, *op. cit.*, pp. 255-6. The Raja's association with the missionaries is too well known to require documentation. Moreover, Dr William Carey wrote to Dr Ryland on July 4, 1822 that the natives "now unite with Europeans, and Europeans with them, in promoting benevolent undertaking without servility on their parts or domination on ours. God is doing great things for India..", vide Eustace Carey, *Memoir of William Carey* (London: Jackson and Walford, 1836), p. 547.

76. This comes out clearly in the work of an American savant, Will Durant, who visited India towards the end of the 1920's while working on his monumental *Story of Civilization.* At around that time the need to justify British rule over India was being keenly felt and in his book *The Case for India* he summarises the British arguments for British Raj in India, acting as the devil's advocate,

so to say. He summarises the case for England under three headings: 1. The Nietzschean Defense; 2. British Contributions to India, and 3. The Key to the White Man's Power. Under the second heading he mentions that "one by one most of the moral abuses have yielded to British patience and suggestion, from the abolition of Suttee in 1829 to the practical ending of child marriage in 1929", vide Will Durant, *The Case for India* (New York: Simon and Schuster, 1930), p. 174. Thus, R. Coupland calls sati a reproach of Hindu society in the beginning (in his *India: A Restatement* [London: Oxford University Press, 1945] p. 4) and in the end (pp. 287-288) makes a sentimental appeal for India's continued membership of the British Commonwealth.

77. Mrs Marcus B. Fuller, *The Wrongs of Indian Womanhood* (New York: Young People's Missionary Movement, 1900), p. 50.

78. Philip Woodruff, *op. cit.*, p. 242.

79. Edward Thompson, *op. cit.*, p. 139. "Is it conceivable that, given opportunity, the submerged root of the matter might come again to life and light?", Katherine Mayo, *Mother India* (New York: Blue Ribbon Books, 1927), p. 84. A British author concluded from a *Times* report (Sept. 1, 1932) of "Indian Widow Rescued from Pyre" that "Our domination in India appears to be slackening its grip with the result that the...account of an attempt to revive this terrible practice appeared", vide Robert J. Blackham, *op. cit.*, p. 204.

80. See Hugh Tinker, *India and Pakistan* (New York: F.A. Praeger, 1962), p. 17.

81. The English expression is patterned on the title of Dara Shikoh's famous Persian work entitled, "The Mingling of the Two Oceans", vide M. Mahfuz-ul-Haq, ed., *Majma-ul-Bahrain* (Calcutta: Asiatic Society of Bengal, 1929).

82. Just as British writers tended to sensationalize sati, Hindu writers tended to *trivialize* it. It was pointed out that sati was not prevalent in the Vedic age (vide A.S. Altekar, *op. cit.*, p. 117), and unknown to the Dharmasūtras (Altekar, p. 119). Furthermore, references from 300 B.C. onwards are not many (Altekar, p. 120) and it was only from 700 A.D. that the rite gained ground (Altekar, p. 126). For the 17th and 18th centuries the percentage of widows committing sati was put at 2% (Altekar, p. 132). Moreover, in the 19th century, though the returns from Bengal were high, the annual averages for the presidencies of Bombay and Madras, the Poona dominion of Peshwa, Central India, and Tanjore district individually were below 50 (Altekar, p. 138). This was only one way in which the issue was trivialized. Two other ways to trivialize it were: to show (a) that its incidence was local, and (b) that its incidence was limited to certain classes. It was thus pointed out that the rite was largely confined to Bengal and Rajputana, and among the Rajputs and the Marathas "who claimed Rajput descent" (Altekar, p. 132). It was thus narrowed down into a martial custom (though Brahmins also took it over; Altekar, p. 116). Also see Ram Gopal, *British Rule in India* (London: Asia Publishing House, 1963), p. 114.

Another Indian reaction to the Western sensationalization of sati was to scandalize Western womanhood. This consisted of a scurrilous attack on Western womanhood as unchaste and therefore, incapable not merely of practising but even understanding a rite such as sati. What Anand K. Coomaraswamy says with dignity, "Indian women do not pinch their feet or waists" (?) ("Sati: A

Defense of the Indian Woman", *The Sociological Review*, April 1913, p. 134), others said with the bluntness of Mill's description of Hindu women (vide James Mill, *op. cit.*, Vol I, p. 321, fn. 2). One of them was Swami Vivekananda who said: "The girls of India would die if they, like American girls, were obliged to expose half their bodies to the vulgar gaze of young men", (Vivekananda, *The Complete Works of Swami Vivekananda*, Vol. III. [Calcutta: Advaita Ashram, 1960] p. 506). This tendency was so widespread in the post-1900 period that it upset Valentine Chirol, *Indian Unrest* (London: Macmillan and Co., 1910), p. 304.

83. A remark made by Vernon Lovell to Edward Thompson, *op. cit.*, p. 129. Also see Philip Woodruff, *op. cit.*, pp. 241-2. "More than any other factor it taught the average Englishman disrespect for the Hindu way of life and thought", Sir Percival Griffiths, *The British Impact on India*, p. 225.

84. Edward Thompson, *op. cit.*, p. 129.

85. Mrs Marcus B. Fuller, op. cit., p. 53. Was W.J. Wilkins' *Modern Hinduism* (London: T. Fisher Unwin, 1887, p. 389) her source? The phrasing is almost identical.

86. Sophia Dobson Collet, *op. cit.*, p. 262. "But the appeal to the Privy Council to annul the new regulation could get only 800 signatures", A.S. Altekar, *op. cit.*, p. 141.

87. Katherine Mayo, *op. cit.*, pp. 82-83.

88. Edward Thompson, *op. cit.*, pp. 77-78; for a different point of view see L.S.S. O'Malley, *Modern India and the West* (London: Oxford University Press, 1968), p. 68.

89. Harry H. Field, *After Mother India* (New York: Harcourt Brace and Co., 1929), p. 106. The statement is quoted as made by an Indian, N. Yagnesvara Sastry, *Stri-Dharma*, July 1928.

90. Predictably, the Indian attitude was to *minimize* the role played by the British. Thus, one can read the essay, "Status of Indian Women" in Ananda K. Coomoraswamy, *The Dance of Shiva* (New York: The Noonday Press, 1957) without ever knowing that Lord William Bentinck abolished sati. He remarks, "coolly", "It was prohibited by law in 1829 on the initiative of Raja Rammohun Roy" (p. 78). Major B.D. Basu says flatly: "If the credit is mainly due to anybody for the abolition of Suttee, it is to Ram Mohun Roy", vide his *Rise of the Christian Power in India*, Vol. IV (Calcutta: R. Chatterjee, 1925), p. 492. It is perhaps interesting to note in this connection that even Karl Marx was aware of the fact that Bentinck's action was a case of action "by individual governors who acted on their own responsibility", vide Shalomo Avineri, *Karl Marx on Colonialism and Modernization* (New York: Anchor Books, 1969) p. 119.

91. P.E. Roberts, *History of British India* (Oxford: Clarendon Press, 1923) p. 303. Unless this writer has overlooked it, the very name of Raja Rammohun Roy is missing from the index, and perhaps from the book? Raja Rammohun surely played a positive role in the abolition of sati vide Sophia Dobson Collet, *op. cit.*, pp. 105-7; Major B.D. Basu, *op. cit.*, p. 492. The tussle for apportioning credit seems to have started as soon as sati was abolished !

92. What made Raja Rammohun Roy such a vigorous advocate of the abolition of sati? One wonders about the relative roles played by (1) his exposure

to the Christian ethic; (2) his association with Moghul Islamic culture; (3) his Śākta maternal background and perhaps, most important of all (4) this domestic tragedy:

> At the death of his eldest brother Jagamohun in 1811 the widow became a Suttee. It is said that Rammohun had endeavoured to persuade her beforehand against this terrible step, but in vain. When, however, she felt the flames she tried to get up and escape from the pile; but her orthodox relations and the priests forced her down with bamboo poles, and kept her there to die, while drums and brazen instruments were loudly sounded to drown her shrieks. Rammohun, unable to save her and filled with unspeakable indignation and pity, vowed within himself then and there that he would never rest until the atrocious custom was rooted out.

See Sophia Dobson Collet, *op. cit.*, pp. 33-34. The influence of European Enlightenment on Raja Rammohun Roy might also constitute a factor to be taken into account in this context.

93. Percival Spear has been accused of not pointing out that:

> the cases of Sati were exceptions rather than the rule and that it had, for some unknown reasons, increased after the British occupation of Bengal. On the contrary he observes that British conscience was so troubled at these barbaric practices that Bentinck abolished Sati. He does not point out that Akbar and some Maratha chiefs had fought against it, or that the Tantrics had denounced it in strong terms...that the Indians under the leadership of Ram Mohun Roy had been asking for its abolition for years.. Without minimising Bentinck's heroic measures historical accuracy demands exposition of full facts.

See D.P. Singhal, *Nationalism in India and Other Historical Essays* (Delhi: Munshiram Manoharlal, 1967), p. 268. Also compare Spear's account with that of Jawaharlal Nehru, *The Discovery of India* (New York: John Day Co., 1946), p. 316.

The "unknown reason" for increase in sati after the British occupation of Bengal may be due to the popular mistaking of the British policy of non-interference in traditional practices as British approval thereof. So the Court of Directors thought anyway: Michael Edwards, *British India* (New York: Taplinger Publishing Co., 1967), p. 101; Sir Percival Griffiths, *op. cit.*, p. 223.

94. Some of the evidence is presented in detail in the next chapter but is capsulized here. Thus, Medhātithi, in his Commentary on the Mānava-Dharma-Śāstra condemns sati as contrary to Vedas, which prohibit suicide, Virāṭa is quoted by Aparārka in his Commentary on the Yajurveda as calling the rite senseless-while alive a widow can at least offer the prescribed oblations, by committing sati she commits sin. Devaṇabhaṭṭa (who lived in South India in the twelfth century) regards sati as an inferior type of Dharma. Six centuries before him the famous Sanskrit author Bāṇa condemns it vehemently. And according to the Tāntra writers anyone responsible for burning a woman-an embodiment of divinity-on the pyre is bound for hell, vide A.S. Altekar, *op. cit.*, pp. 124-5, wherein the Sanskrit originals are also quoted. A.L. Basham also acknowledges that sati "was condemned by the humane poet Bāṇa, in the 7th century, and by the Tantric sects" (*The Wonder that was India* [New York: Grove Press Inc., 1959,] p. 188).

The efforts of the Moghuls apart, the Marathas viewed the rite with displeasure. Unfortunately, as Edward Thompson says, they have had a "bad press" with the British writers. Thus, Queen Ahalya Bai was opposed to sati. It was banned in the Peshwa's personal dominions and in Tanjore and had been abolished in the Marāṭhā state of Savantvadi already by 1810; vide Edward Thompson, *op. cit.*, pp. 58-59.

Another fact which came to be overlooked was that the Regulation of 1829 was passed "in spite of the opposition of many leading Hindus *and of some Englishmen*" (J.N. Farquhar, *Modern Religious Movements in India* [Delhi: Munshiram Manoharlal, 1967] p. 401, emphasis added). To recognize that even some Englishmen had been opposed to the abolition of sati (rather than to sati) for whatever reason, could be embarrassing? It is worth noting, however, that Lord Bentinck himself exonerated Brooke, Ewer, Courtney Smith, etc., who had opposed the abolition of sati. "I should have acted as they...", vide H.H. Dodwell, ed., *The Cambridge History of India*, Vol. VI (Delhi: S. Chand and Co., 1964), p. 143.

Some Western writers also noticed this tendency to give a lopsided account of sati. Henry Noel Brailsford wrote *Subject India* (New York: John Day Co., 1943) because "he had certain things to say which no one else is saying" (above, p. viii). In his comments on sati he proceeded to say things which no one else seemed to be saying, viz., that "burning heretics—an exclusively Christian rite" was a common practice in Europe and that an English woman was roasted alive in 1685. The manner in which the Tudor monarch Henry VIII disposed of his wives could also have been mentioned. A similar attitude appeared and continues to show in Indian writings. When Western writers sometimes tend to *particularize* sati to India or when they try to establish its unique prevalence in India as particularly horrible (Edward Thompson, *op. cit.*, pp. 132-4), then, as if in response, Indian writers tend to *universalize* the issue and cite incidents of widow-burning or excessive cruelty from other cultures, vide R.C. Majumdar, ed., *op. cit.*, Part II, p. 268, etc.

95. Mrs Marcus B. Fuller, *op. cit.*, p. 53.

96. Philip Woodruff, *op. cit.*, p. 258. Some authors were frankly apologetic but apologetically frank-"It may seem offensive to suggest that there is still any sympathy with this practice amongst those classes who are bound to take a continually larger part in the ruling of India, but it is necessary to face the unpleasant fact that the ancient rite had never troubled the Hindu conscience in the least", G.T. Garratt, *op. cit.*, p. 235.

97. Edward Thompson, *op. cit.*, p. 143.

98. Sati, in fact, had been used as a justification for British Rule even in earlier times, even when this need for justifying British Raj was not that keenly felt, vide A.T. Embree, *Charles Grant and British Rule in India* (New York: Columbia University Press, 1962), p. 157. Even Raja Rammohun Roy said in this connection, "India requires many years of British domination", vide Amaury de Riencourt, *op. cit.*, p. 230.

But in later times, with the Curzonian realization, "As long as we rule India, we are the greatest power in the world. If we lost it, we shall drop straightaway to a third rate" (quoted by B.N. Pandey, *op. cit.*, p. 1), and with the growing unrest which manifested itself during Curzon's reign, the need for justifying British Raj was all the more keenly felt, even more keenly than in the immediate post-Mutiny period.

99. Philip Woodruff, *The Men Who Ruled India*, Vol. II (New York: St. Martin's Press, 1954), Chp. 2.

100. Edward Thompson, *op. cit.*, p. 144.

101. *Ibid.*, p. 143.

102. *Ibid.*, p. 129.

103. J.N. Farquhar shows empathy, even sympathy, for the sati view. He even quotes a passage in a metre most often associated with Tennyson and remarks, "With the love and self-devotion of the Sati we can deeply sympathise. How many broken-hearted widows and widowers have prayed for easeful deaths !". But his attitude is tempered by the fact that "these tragic glooms and awful ordeals...be imposed as laws upon weak women", vide J.N. Farquhar's *The Crown of Hinduism* (London: Oxford University Press, 1913), p. 100. Thus, he stops far short of Edwin Arnold's soulful endorsement above.

104. Sir George Macmunn, *The Religions and Hidden Cults of India* (London: Sampson Low, 1931), p. 174.

105. Quoted in Harendranath Maitra, *Hinduism: The World Ideal* (New York: Dodd, Mead and Co., 1916), p. 117. This attitude is strongly criticised by Edward Thompson whose impulse to write his book "dates back to my shame and anger in India when men and women of my own race extolled Suttee" (Preface).

One of the apologetic patterns of Hindu response against Western attacks was to extol sati, vide Anand K. Coomaraswamy, *The Dance of Shiva* pp. 98-123. This attitude on the part of Hindus came in for severe criticism at the hands of Swami Vivekananda, see *The Complete Works of Swami Vivekananda*, Vol. IV (Calcutta: Advaita Ashram, 1955), p. 491.

106. See Monier Williams, *op. cit.*, p. 258, fn. 2: Edward Thompson, *op. cit.*, pp. 16-17; A.S. Altekar, *op. cit.*, pp. 117-118, etc.

107. Vincent A. Smith, *op. cit.*, p. 665. Vincent Smith's remarks on Sati are of great interest. He has been regarded as an "imperialist" historian even by Western scholars, e.g., by A.L. Basham, vide C.H. Philips, ed., *Historians of India, Pakistan and Ceylon* (London: Oxford University Press, 1961). His account of sati, however, is surprisingly un-imperialistic. The closest he comes to patting the British Raj over it is that "the legislation of Lord William Bentinck may claim credit for having affected a definite improvement in Hinduism" (*op. cit.*, p. 664). Otherwise, he mentions prohibition by Maratha princes, which is remarkable as Smith is notorious in Indian circles for having branded the Hindu hero Shivaji as a robber (*op. cit.*, p. 435). He also mentions its prohibition by the Portuguese (*op. cit.*, p. 666) and presents a remarkably balanced account for one reputed to be an imperialist historian par excellence.

108. N.M. Penzer, *op. cit.*, pp. 255-258.

109. Edward B. Tylor, *Primitive Culture*, Vol. I (Boston: Estes and Lauriat, 1874), pp. 463-5.

110. Edward Thompson, *op. cit.*, p. 26.

111. Edward B. Tylor, *op. cit.*, p. 466.

112. *Ibid.*, p. 466.

113. This admiration has largely been male admiration. Why, it might be asked, was there no rite of the husband immolating himself on the wife's death? Not that no poet thought of it. Kālidāsa did. The Raghuvaṁśa (VIII-72) says that if Aja, on the death of his beloved wife Indumatī "did not consign his body to flames with his queen" it was "not because he cared for his life but because he apprehended the scandal that the king...died after his queen from grief", vide. G.B. Nandargikar, *The Raghuvaṁśa of Kālidāsa* (Bombay: Radhabhai Atmaram Sagoon, 1897), p. 247. The King finally dies out of grief (above, pp. 256-257).

114. Sati has been a factor in apologetic patterns on both sides in the Indo-Western encounter. The sharp Western Christian criticism of the barbarity of the rite made Hinduism develop an apologetic attitude towards sati. Later, when strident nationalist criticism of British Raj put the West on the defensive, sati was used as a part of the Western apologia for justifying British rule over India.

115. An effort has been made to interpret sati even along Freudian lines, vide P. Spratt, *Hindu Culture and Personality* (Bombay: Manaktalas, 1966), p. 71.

116. Edward Thompson, *op. cit.*, p. 145.

117. Percival Griffiths (*op. cit.*, p. 217), speaks of "the irreconcilable antagonism of the Hindu and the European wives on this subject. By the good Hindu, the woman who gave this last proof of devotion was greatly venerated and was recognised to have acquired great merit; whereas to the Englishman, and indeed to the Christian generally, the practice could not be but profoundly repugnant".

In the light of the paper, this is perhaps an overstatement. It has been shown how there existed a Hindu tradition of criticism of sati; it has also been shown how there was some admiration for sati even among Englishmen. It would, therefore, probably be more accurate to say that whereas in the Hindu mix of admiration and condemnation, condemnation took a remote second place, it was the opposite with Western reaction—condemnation predominated with an occasional streak of admiration.

Percival Griffiths' remarks also open the space for some closing reflections on the role of sati in Indian historiography. As Percival Spear (*op. cit.*, p. 447) points out, Indian history can be viewed with the eyes of an Indian, a Pakistani or a British historian. Each will look differently at sati. Percival Griffiths' position is that of a British historian. He joins hands with Edward Thomspon (*op. cit.*, p. 131) whom he quotes, in maintaining that sati prevented natives "from taking a larger share in the government of the country", Percival Griffiths, *op. cit.*, p. 225. It thus justifies what Indians regarded as British tardiness in granting self-government. The Pakistani historian would probably emphasise the fact that sati was least practised in those regions which were under direct Muslim rule (vide E. Thompson, *op. cit.*, p. 57). The Indian or more specifically the Hindu historians would, perhaps, "commonly blame Mahammadan lawlessness; women were unsafe, and it was best to preserve their honour by burning them when their protectors died. It is usual to blame bad Hindu custom on to Mahommadanism", E. Thompson, *op. cit.*, p. 48.

118. We ignore here the fact that some law-books, such as that of Manu, are

silent about sati (see P.V. Kane, *History of Dharmaśāstra*, Vol. II Pt. I [Poona: Bhandarkar Oriental Research Institute, 1941] p. 626; A.S. Altekar, *The Position of Women in Hindu Civilization* [Patna: Motilal Banarsidass, 1973] p. 122), while others, such as that of Viṣṇu mention it but do not recommend it (*ibid.*, Delhi: Motilal Banarsidass, 1965 p. 117).

119. A.S. Altekar, *op. cit.*, p. 120, fn. 4.

120. P.V. Kane, *op. cit.*, p. 628.

121. A.S. Altekar, *op. cit.*, p. 124.

122. As quoted in Benjamin Walker, *The Hindu World*, Vol. II (New York: Frederick A. Praeger, 1968) p. 464; also see A.S. Altekar. *op. cit.*, p. 124; P.V. Kane, *op. cit.*, p. 628.

123. P.V. Kane, *op. cit.*, pp. 631-632.

124. *Ibid.*, p. 627.

125. *Ibid.*, pp. 627, 634.

126. A.S. Altekar, *op. cit.*, p. 124.

127. *Ibid.*, p. 124.

128. P.V. Kane, *op. cit.*, p. 633. Prof. Indra refers to the fact that several Smṛti writers "make self-immolation alternative to lifelong asceticism for a widow" and adds "The author of the Mitakshara whose authority is always to be respected, has also decided on the subject of concremation in a similar manner. Says he, 'The widow, who is not desirous of final beatitude, but who wishes for only a limited term of a small degree of future fruition is authorized to accompany her husband'" (*op. cit.*, p. 117 and fn. 2). It appears, however, that Vijñāneśvara, the author of Mitākṣarā, is more deeply committed in favour of sati than the above passage would lead one to believe (see P.V. Kane, *op. cit.*, pp. 631, 632).

129. T.M.P. Mahadevan, *Outlines or Hinduism* (Bombay: Chetana Ltd., 1960), p. 205.

130. *Ibid.*

131. A.S. Altekar, *op. cit.*, p. 125.

132. Benjamin Walker captures a sense of the verses overlooked by Altekar above "that a woman who burnt herself, "*howsoever noble her motives,* would surely go to hell" (*op. cit.*, Vol. II, p. 464 emphasis added).

133. See Edward Thompson, *op. cit.*, pp. 58-59.

133a. Raymond Brady Williams, *A New Face of Hinduism: The Swaminarayan Religion* (Cambridge: Cambridge University Press, 1984), pp. 21-22, 143.

134. See Ananda K. Coomaraswamy, *op. cit.*, pp. 109-115, passim.

135. W. Norman Brown, *The United States and India and Pakistan* (Harvard University Press, 1963) p. 25.

136. For a description of this sati see N.M. Penzer, *op. cit.*, p. 261; for actual text as translated from Greek see R.C. Majumdar, ed., *The Age of Imperial Unity* (Bombay: Bharatiya Vidya Bhavan, 153) pp. 567-8.

137. Ananda K. Coomaraswamy, *op. cit.*, p. 111.

138. An error for way?

139. Ananda K. Coomaraswamy, *op. cit.*, pp. 111-112.

140. Quoted in Harendranath Maitra, *op. cit.*, p. 117

141. Edward Thompson, *op. cit.*

142. *Ibid.*, Preface

143. R.C. Majumdar, H.C. Raychaudhuri and Kalikinkar Datta, *An Advanced History of India* (London: Macmillan & Co., 1948) pp. 400, 496.

144. *Ibid.*, pp. 822-5

145. See Ram Chandra Prasad, *Early English Travellers in India* (Delhi: Motilal Banarsidass, 1965) p. 57, 118, 264, 292, 340 etc.

146. *Ibid.*, p. 118

147. *Ibid.*, p. 268, emphasis added.

148. See P.J. Marshall, ed., *op. cit.*, p. 116 etc.

149. Aziz Ahmad, *Studies in Islamic Culture in the Indian Environment* (Oxford: Clarendon Press, 1964) p. 118.

150. A.L. Basham, *The Wonder that was India* (New York: Hawthorn Books, 1963) p. 189.

151. Ananda Coomaraswamy, *op. cit.*, p. 109; also see Pandurang Vaman Kane, op. cit., Vol. II Part I, p. 636. P.V. Kane writes:

"Modern India does not justify the practice of *sati*, but it is a warped mentality that rebukes modern Indians for expressing admiration and reverence for the cool and unfaltering courage of Indian women in becoming *satis* or performing the *jauhar* for cherishing their ideals of womanly conduct. If Englishmen can feel pride in their ancestors who grabbed one fourth of the world's surface or if Frenchmen can feel pride in the deeds of their Emperor Napoleon who tried to enslave the whole of Europe and yet are not held up to ridicule or rebuke, there is no reason why poor Indians cannot express admiration for the sacrifices which their women made in the past, though they may condemn the institution itself which demanded such terrible sacrifice and suffering."

152. *Ibid.*, p. 625.

153. *Ibid.*, pp. 625-6.

154. P.V. Kane, *op. cit.*, Vol I Part I, p. 583.

155. R.C. Majumdar, ed., *The Struggle for Empire* (Bombay: Bharatiya Vidya Bhavan, 1966) p. 295, fn. 1.

156. P.V. Kane, *op. cit.*, Vol. II Part I, p. 627.

157. A.S. Altekar, *op. cit.*, p. 124.

158. *Ibid.*

159. P.V. Kane, *op. cit.*, Vol. II Part I, p. 628.

160. See Neeta Sharma, *Bāṇabhaṭṭa: A Literary Study* (Delhi: Munshiram Manoharlal, 1968) p. 106.

161. See A.S. Altekar, *op. cit.*, pp. 124-5.

162. Upendra Nath Ball, *Rammohun Roy* (Calcutta: U. Ray and Sons, 1933) p. 6.

163. Sushil Chaudhury, 'A note on 'Sati' in Medieval India' in *Indian Historical Congress Proceedings* 1964 (Aligarh: Indian Historical Congress, 1967) Part II Section II, pp. 75-83.

163a. *Ibid.*, p. 75.

163b. *Ibid.*, p. 83.

164. Ananda K. Coomaraswamy, op. cit., p. 111, emphasis added.

165. *Ibid.*, p. 111.

166. *Ibid.*, pp. 111-112, emphasis added.

167. See J.A.B. van Buitenen, *The Mahābhārata* Volume I (Chicago University Press, 1973), p. 260.

168. P.P.S. Sastri, ed., *The Mahābhārata* Vol. I Part I (Madras: V. Ramaswamy Sastrulu & Sons, 1931), 767-772.

169. Epigraphic evidence seems to be silent on the question of Brāhmaṇas but indicates that relatives tried to dissuade the widow (see P.V. Kane, op. cit., Vol. II, Part I, p. 635.

170. William Johns, *op. cit.*, p. 8.

171. *Ibid.*, p. 10.

172. "Who are the nobles", *ibid.*

173. *Ibid.*, pp. 10-11.

174. *Ibid.*, p. 13.

175. But see Rev. Mr Lord's account above.

176. William Johns, *op. cit.*, p. 5.

177. *Ibid.*, p. 15.

178. *Ibid.*, passim. It is true that the tract referred to here by William Johns is a product of missionary zeal, and that some of the accounts are by missionaries as well, and hence their prejudice should be properly discounted. Yet Tavernier and Bernier had hardly any missionary axe to grind; and some of the gruesome details of sati are confirmed by Indian sources (vide Upendra Nath Ball. *op. cit.* p. 79), so that the picture presented above would seem to be fairly accurate. Also see Sushil Chaudhury, *op. cit.*, pp. 78-79.

179. See R.C. Majumdar, H.C. Raychaudhuri, Kalikinkar Datta, *op. cit.*, p. 1016.

180. Sachchidananda Bhattacharya, *A Dictionary of Indian History* (New York: George Brazilier, 1967), p. 128.

181. In this context the remarks made by both Max Müller and Kaegi on the role of the *brāhmanas* in the commission of sati seem to show a lack of historical awareness of this change. On the alteration of *agre* into *agne* in Ṛg Veda X. 18.7 Max Müller remarks: "This is perhaps the most flagrant instance of what can be done by an unscrupulous priesthood. Here have thousands of lives been sacrificed, and a practical rebellion threatened on the authority of a passage which was mangled, mistranslated and misapplied." (quoted by P. Thomas, *Indian Women Through the Ages* [London: Asian Publishing House, 1964] p. 234). The statement seems to be more true for the medieval than the ancient period of Hindu history. The same seems to apply to Kaegi's comment: "The well-known custom of burning of widows for thousands of years demanded by the Brahmanas, is nowhere evidenced in the Rigveda; only by palpable falsification of a hymn has the existence of the custom been forcibly put into the texts which on the contrary, prove directly the opposite, i.e. the return of the widow from her husband's corpse into a happy life and her remarriage" (quoted in Indra, *The Status of Women in Ancient India* [Delhi: Motilal Banarsidass, 1955] p. 116). It is interesting to note that the alleged misreading which draws heavy fire from Max Müller and Kaegi "can be traced to Raghunandan, Cr. 1500 A.D. and no further" (Charles Rockwell Lanman, *A Sanskrit Reader* [Harvard University Press, 1971] p. 382) and even in his case "it must be admitted that either the mss. are corrupt or Raghunandana committed an innocent slip" (P.V. Kane, *op. cit.*, Vol. II Part I p. 634).

182. See A.S. Altekar, *op. cit.*, p. 128; P. Thomas, *op. cit.*, p. 231; Indra, *op. cit.*, p. 119; P.V. Kane, *op. cit.*, Vol. II, Pt. I p. 630; etc.

183. A.S. Altekar, *op. cit.*, p. 128; also see P. Thomas, *op. cit.*, p. 231.

184. Indra, *op. cit.*, p. 119.

185. P.V. Kane, *op. cit.*, p. 627; also see note 1468. The Miṭākṣarā, however, regards *anvārohaṇa* as the common duty of all castes (ibid., p. 631).

186. P.V. Kane, *op. cit.*, p. 627.

187. "Soon after 1000 A.D." (A.S. Altekar, *op. cit.*, p. 129).

188. A.S. Altekar, *op. cit.*, p. 129.

189. *Ibid.*, p. 129

190. P.V. Kane, *op. cit.*, p. 627.

191. R.C. Majumdar, H.C. Raychaudhuri and Kaliknikar Datta, *op. cit.*, pp. 822-825; A.S. Altekar, *op. cit.*, pp. 117, 140 f.

192. T.M.P. Mahadevan, *op. cit.*, p. 28; but also see K. Satchidananda Murty, *Revelation and Reason in Advaita Vedānta* (New York: Columbia University Press, 1959) p. 50.

193. It should be noted, however, that "None of the Dharmasūtras except Viṣṇu contains any reference to sati" (Panduranga Vaman Kane, *op. cit.*, Vol. II Part I pp. 625-6). The position of the Viṣṇusmṛti may also be mentioned here. "Viṣṇusmṛti (C. 100 A.D.) thinks the custom is not illogical; it advanced the view that in spite of diversity of Karman, a widow can, though other relations cannot, go the way of the departed soul by dying after him. Viṣṇu himself does not recommend it; he merely mentions it. He is in fact one of the earliest to recognise the widow as an heir to her husband; he allows her to remarry also" (A.S. Altekar, *op. cit.*, pp. 122-3).

194. *Ibid.*, p. 633. However, "The Śuddhitattva remarks that this extreme or sweeping statement is made by way of belauding *sahamaraṇa*" (*ibid.*).

195. A.S. Altekar points out that this passage, to which he refers as IV. 31-32 "is an interpolation, because two verses earlier, Parāśara permits a widow to remarry" (*op. cit.*, p. 126). "Medhatithi takes notice of Angiras but not Parashara, as enjoining Anumarana. Parashara texts on Anumarana may therefore be interpolations" (Indra, *op. cit.*, p. 119, fn. 3).

196. It should be borne in mind here that "there were old commentators who were opposed to the practice of *satī*" (Pandurang Vaman Kane, *op. cit.*, p. 631).

197. Indra, *op. cit.*, p. 117.

198. P.V. Kane, *op. cit.*, p. 631.

199. *Ibid.*

200. *Ibid.*, p. 633.

201. *Ibid.*

202. *Ibid.*, p. 627.

203. *Ibid.*, pp. 628, 626.

204. Pandurang Vaman Kane, *op. cit.*, pp. 626-627. In the Mahābhārata, Uttarā, the widow of Abhimanyu is not shown as committing Suttee. "We, however, find Uttarā represented as burning herself with her husband Abhimanyu in the Bali island version of the *Mahābhārata*. The reason for the discrepancy is obvious; the Bali island version belongs to a time when the custom

of Sati had become popular" (A.S. Altekar, *op. cit.*, p. 120, fn. 4). It may also be noted that Madhva attributes some verses in support of sati to "the *Mahābhārata* at Parāśara IV. 33; they, however, do not occur in the epic" (*ibid.*, p. 126, fn. 4). Again "the Mahābhārata is unaware of any Yādava widows having burnt themselves on their husband's funeral pyres; according to the *Padmapurāṇa*, however, all of them become Satīs (Uttarakāṇḍa, Chap. 279)" (*ibid.*, p. 122).

205. *Ibid.*, p. 626. Once, however, the practice took root it would have been possible to indirectly justify it through the Manusmṛti as "Manu IV. 178 asks people to do whatever their forefathers did" (*ibid.*, p. 630).

206. *Ibid.*, pp. 631-632. It may be noted that "Medhatithi (900 A.D.), a commentator on Manu Samhita holds Angiras responsible for according first legal sanction to the evil custom of Anumarana, which he himself condemns in no unmistakable terms as an act of suicide, which can be tolerated only as Apad-dharma—a transgression pardonable in times of distress. Vijnaneshwar (1100 A.D.) and Madhvacharya who wrote a gloss on the Parashara Samhita on the other hand, hold Anumarana as a Dharma and not an act of suicide. Evidently the whole mental vision had changed between the times when Medhatithi and Vijnaneshwar respectively wrote, that is between the ninth and the eleventh centuries" (Indra, *op. cit.*, p. 119).

207. P.V. Kane, *op. cit.*, p. 628 note 1472.

208. *Ibid.*, pp. 618-619.

209. Charles Rockwell Lanman, *op. cit.*, p. 86.

210. P.V. Kane, *op. cit.*, p. 617.

211. Charles Rockwell Lanman, *op. cit.*, pp. 382-383. A.S. Altekar points out that "Even when the last word is changed into *agneḥ*, it is only a forced construction that can detect in this stanza a reference to the widow immolation" (*op. cit.*, p. 117). On the alleged role of Raghunandana in instituting the change P.V. Kane remarks: "The Śuddhitattva as printed is corrupt but it appears that it read the last quarter of Rg. X.18.7 as 'ārohantu jalayonim-agne' (let them ascend the watery seat or origin, O fire !) meaning probably 'may fire be to them as cool as water'. Some writers have charged the brāhmaṇa priesthood (or Raghunandana) with having purposely changed the reading of the verse Ṛg. X.18.7 in order to make it suit the rite of immolating oneself in fire (i.e. 'agne' or 'agneḥ' was substituted for 'agre'). But this charge is not sustainable. That the verse Ṛg. X.18.7 as it actually is was held to refer to widow burning centuries before Raghunandana follows from the fact that even the Brahmapurāṇa and Aparāka (quoted above on p. 628) take it in that sense. It was therefore not necessary to alter the reading. Further, even if some priests or Raghunandana had changed it, that fact would have been detected in no time, as in those days there were thousands of people who knew every syllable of the ṚgVeda by heart. Therefore it must be admitted that either the mss. are corrupt or Raghunandana committed an innocent slip. That mantra was not addressed to widows at all, but to ladies of the deceased man's household whose husbands were living and the Gṛhyasūtra of Āśv. made use of it with that meaning. Raghunandana, a profound student of dharmaśāstras and smṛtis (and often styled Smārta-bhaṭṭācārya), could not have been ignorant of what Āśv. said." (*op. cit.*, p. 634).

212. A.A. Macdonell, *The Vedic Mythology* (Varanasi: Indological Book House, 1971) p. 167. Read RV X.188.9 as RV X.18.8-9.

213. A.A. Macdonell, *A History of Sanskrit Literature* (London: William Heinemann, 1913) pp. 125-126.

214. Bhagwat Saran Upadhyay, *Women in Ṛgveda* (Benares: Nand Kishose & Bros., 1941) p. 97.

215. P.V. Kane, *op. cit.*, p. 625 note 1462. A.S. Altekar also observes: "It was also argued that a passage in the Aukhya Śākhā of the *Saṁhitā* quoted in the 84th *anuvāka* of the *Nārāyaṇīya Taittirīya Upanishad* refers to a prayer by a widow to god Fire that she was about to follow the *anugamana-vrata* or the Satī custom and that she may be able to bear the ordeal and reap the promised reward. The *Nārāyāṇīya-upanishad* is however a late work; the passage from the Aukhya Śākhā quoted in it is otherwise not known to us from any other source. We cannot therefore conclude from it that the Satī custom was recognized as a ritual in the Vedic period" (*op. cit.*, pp. 117-118).

216. Indra, *op. cit.*, pp. 115-116.

217. William Dwight Whitney, *Atharva-Veda-Saṁhitā* Vol. II (Delhi: Motilal Banarsidass, 1971) p. 848.

218. *Ibid.*

219. *Indra,* op. cit., p. 116.

220. Satī or sati (Skt. *sati,* lit., good woman, fem. of *sat, sant,* existing, true, good,—more at *sooth*) 1: the act or custom of a Hindu widow willingly cremating herself or being cremated on the funeral pyre of her husband as an indication of devotion to him. 2: a woman cremated in this way. (*Webster's Third New International Dictionary* [Springfield, Mass., G. & C. Merriam and Co., 1959] p. 2306).

221. See William Crooke, ed., *op. cit.*

222. N.M. Penzer, ed., *op. cit.*, Vol. IV, p. 258.

223. P.V. Kane, *op. cit*, Vol. II, Pt. II, p. 627-628.

224. *Ibid.*

225. *Ibid.*, p. 628.

226. *Ibid.*

227. Benjamin Walker, *op. cit.*, Vol., II, p. 462; etc.

228. See P.V. Kane, ed., *The Harshacarita of Bāṇabhaṭṭa* (Delhi: Motilal Banarsidass, 1973), pp. v-xii.

229. For comparison with Rati see *ibid.*, pp. 100-101.

230. *Ibid.*, p. 101

231. E.B. Cowell and F.W. Thomas, trs., *The Harṣa-carita of Bāṇa* (Delhi: Motilal Banarsidass, 1961), p. 154.

232. *Ibid.*, p. 155.

233. Pandurang Vaman Kane, *op. cit.*, Vol. II Part 1, p. 628.

234. E.B. Cowell and F.W. Thomas, *op. cit.*, p. 156, fn. 6.

235. It may be noted that the "original" Satī "destroyed herself by fire, but in this case, though she proved herself a faithful wife, she did not burn herself with her husband's body" (W.J. Wilkins, *Modern Hinduism* [London: T. Fisher Unwin, 1887] p. 377). In that case, however, the wife died, but not the husband; in Yaśomatī's case both the husband and the wife die but the wife dies

beforehand. It may be noted that the royal physician, a close friend of Harṣa, out of despair himself entered the fire at not being able to save the king before the king died (vide E.B. Cowell and F.W. Thomas, tr., *op. cit.*, p. 145). Thus this instance qualifies as an example of "*sati* immolation which is not *satī*" (see Pandurang Vaman Kane, *op. cit.*, Vol. II Part I, p. 629).

236. Percival Spear, ed., *The Oxford History of India* (Oxford: Clarendon Press, 1967), pp. 651-652. H.H. Dodwell, ed., *The Cambridge History of India*, Vol. VI (Cambridge University Press, 1932), pp. 102-3, etc.

237. Percival Spear, ed., *op. cit.*, p. 837. H.H. Dodwell, ed., *op. cit.*, p. 549, etc.

238. H.H. Dodwell, ed. *op. cit.*, p. 549.

239. "Not since the abolition of sati in 1829 had so sensitive an area of Hindu social custom been threatened by the legislative arm of the government of British India as on January 9, 1891, when Sir Andrew Slobb first moved his bill to raise the marriageable age of consent" (Stanley A. Wolpert, *Tilak and Gokhale: Revolution and Reform in the Making of Modern India* [University of California Press, 1962], p. 65).

240. See Ananda K. Coomaraswamy, *op. cit.*, p. 110; W. Norman Brown, *op. cit.*, p. 56., etc.

241. Upendra Nath Ball, *op. cit.*, p. 92.

242. *Ibid.*, pp. 92-93. Also see Sophia Dobson Collet, *op.*, *cit.*, pp. 255-6.

243. See Upendra Nath Ball, *op. cit.*, p. 93.

244. *Ibid.*, p. 97.

245. *Ibid.*, pp. 97-98. Also see R.C. Majumdar, ed., *British Paramountcy and Indian Renaissance*, Part II (Bombay: Bharatiya Vidya Bhavan, 1965), p. 276.

246. See Upendra Nath Ball, *op. cit.*, p. 103, emphasis added.

247. *Ibid.*, pp. 103-4.

248. *Mahratta* (May 29, 1881), p. 1; quoted by Stanley A. Wolpert, *op. cit.*, p. 47. "His greatest objection to the Bill was that it gave officials of a foreign race the chance to interfere in the religious life and beliefs of Hindu society. He looked at the bill as the thin edge of the wedge which would eventually break up the social and religious independence of the Hindus, and was horrified at the idea that an ancient community should in this way be deprived of its religious as well as its political independence (D.V. Tahmankar, *Lokamanya Tilak* [London: John Murray, 1956,] p. 46).

249. *Kesari*, March 24, 1891, p. 3, quoted by Stanley A. Wolpert, *op. cit.*, p. 60.

250. Ram Gopal, *Lokamanya Tilak* (New Delhi: Asia Publishing House, 1956), p. 64; but see Stanley A. Wolpert, *op. cit.*, p. 52.

251. *Ibid.*

252. One difference, however, may be noted. While Raja Rammohun Roy was opposed to *direct* governmental interference he proposed *indirect* governmental dissuasion of sati, alongside efforts within the Hindu society to do away with it; Bal Gangadhar Tilak opposed direct governmental interference like Raja Rammohun Roy and wanted the reform to come from within like him, but would not perhaps approve of even an indirect British role in the matter.

253. See Theodore L. Shay, *The Legacy of the Lokamanya* (Oxford University Press, 1956), passim.

254. R.C. Majumdar, ed., *op. cit.*, p. 584.

255. *Ibid.*, Chapter IX passim.

256. T.V. Parvate, *Bal Gangadhar Tilak* (Ahmedabad: Navajivan Publishing House, 1958), p. 41. This is comparable to the actions of the orthodox party after the abolition of sati which too were unsuccessful.

257. See D.P. Karmarkar, *Bal Gangadhar Tilak* (Bombay: Popular Book Dept., 1956), p. 44.

258. R.C. Majumdar, ed., *op. cit.*, Chapter XV.

259. R.C. Majumdar, ed., *op. cit.*, pp. 6, 11-12, and 581-2.

260. *Ibid.*, pp. 576-585.

261. Iqbal Singh, *Rammohun Roy*, Vol. I (New Delhi: Asia Publishing House, 1958), p. 191.

262. D.V. Tahmankar, *op. cit.*, p. 45.

263. R.C. Majumdar, ed., *op. cit.*, pp. 4-5.

264. D.V. Tahmankar, *op. cit.*, p. 48.

265. *Calcutta Journal*, 20 January 1820.

266. John Clark Marshman, *The Life and Times of Carey, Marshman and Ward* (London: 1859), Vol. 1, p. 180.

267. *Friend of India* (monthly series), Oct. 1819, p. 473-76.

268. *Regulation XVII of* 1829, preamble.

269. Rammohun Roy's letter to John Digby, dated 18 January 1828 in *The English Works of Raja Rammohun Roy* (Calcutta: 1947), Pt. 4, p. 96.

270. Rammohun Roy, *The Practice of Burning Widows Alive* (Calcutta: 1818), advertisement.

271. Ibid., p. 96.

272. Bentinck's minute; in Demetrius Charles de Kavanagh Boulger, *Lord William Bentinck* (Oxford: Clarendon Press, 1892).

273. *Sambada Bhaskara*, 26 May 1849. Translated by the author.

274. *Calcutta Gazette*, Monday 27 June 1831.

275. Reginald Heber, *Narrative of a Journey Through the Upper Provinces of India* (London: 1961), Vol. 1, p. 48.

276. Rammohun Roy, *op. cit.*, p. 97.

277. Demetrius Charles de Kavanagh Boulger, *op. cit.*

278. *Ibid.*

279. Frederick John Shore, *Notes on Indian Affairs* (London: 1837), Vol. 2, p.

280. *Bengal: Past & Present*, V. 94, pt. 2, no. 179, July/Dec. 1975.

281. C.H. Tawney (tr.), *The Ocean of Story* (London: 1924), Vol. 4, Appendix I.

282. *Calcutta Gazette*, 18 January 1830. Letter on the Hindus to Bentinck.

283. Abbe J.A. Dubois, *Hindu Manners, Customs and Ceremonies.* (3rd ed.: Oxford: Clarendon Press, 1947), p. 367.

284. Claudius Buchanan, "The Star in the East with Three new Sermons", in *The Works of the Rev. Claudius Buchanan* (New York, 1812), p. 334.

285. *Ibid.*

286. Claudius Buchanan "Memoir of the Expediency of an Ecclesiastical Establishment for British India" in *op. cit.*, p. 217.

287. *Ibid.*

288. S. Pearce Carey, *William Carey* (5th ed.; London: 1924), p. 176.

289. *Ibid.*, p. 177.

290. *Ibid.*, p. 209.

291. John Clark Marshman, *op. cit.*, p. 222.

292. "Extract Judicial Consultations, 7 February, 1805" in G.B. *Parliament. Papers Relating to East India Affairs, viz. Hindoo Widows, and Voluntary Immolations.* v. 1, p. 24.

293. Reginald Heber, *op. cit.*, Vol. 1, p. 47.

294. *Ibid.*, p. 48.

295. *Ibid.*

296. *Ibid.*

297. *Ibid.*

298. *Ibid.*

299. G.B. *Parliament.* H. of C. Debates. v. 26, June 22, 1813, col. 862.

300. *Missionary Register*, 1820, p. 120; 1821, p. 116; and *Missionry Papers* nos. II, XXVI, XXXII, XXXIV, quoted in Kenneth Ingham, *Reformers in India*, 1793-1833 (Cambridge: Cambridge Unibersity Press, 1956), p. 48.

301. William Ward, *A View of the History, Literature and Religion of the Hindoos* (3rd ed.; London: 1817), Vol. 2, p. 104.

302. John Clark Marshman, *op. cit.*, Vol. 2, p. 245.

303. *Ibid.*, p. 246.

304. The first ed. was thus reviewed in *The World* (July 29, 1829)—"This volume furnishes on this subject (the safety of the abolition of sati), and on the several subjects to which its title-page refers, the most accurate and ample information...We beseech our readers to acquaint themselves with his statements and to let no opportunity be neglected of advancing his benevolent aim". James Pegg, *India's Cries to British Humanity...* (2nd ed.; London: 1830), p. xii.

305. *Friend of India* (Monthly series), Oct. 1819, p. 473-76.

306. John Clark Marshman, *op. cit.*, Vol. 1, p. 180.

307. Constitution of the Dharma Sabha.

308. Bentinck's letter to Astell, 12 January 1829, in C.H. Philips, (ed.) *The Correspondence of Lord William Cavendish Bentinck* (Oxford: Oxford University Press, 1977), p. 140.

309. John Clark Marshman, *op. cit.*, Vol. 2, p. 413.

310. Fanny Parkes, *Wanderings of a Pilgrim in Search of the Picturesque* (London: 1850), Vol. 1, p. 162.

311. Bentinck's minute on sati (8 Nov. 1829) in C.H. Philips, ed., *op. cit.*, Vol. I, p. 344.

312. Maria (Dundas) Graham Calcott, *Letters on India* (London: 1814), p. 284.

313. W.H. Sleeman, *Rambles and Recollections of an Indian Official* (Rev. ed.; London: 1915), p. 337.

314. Rammohun Roy, *op. cit.*, p. 97.

315. It could be argued that the Anglicised form Suttee be preferred to the Sanskrit form Satī because the use of the word sati to denote the practice, when it really stands for a person, is not in keeping with correct usage. But it is now customary to do so.

316. Percival Spear (ed.), *The Oxford History of India* (Oxford: Clarendon Press, 1985), pp. 454, 576; M.A. Laird (ed.), *Bishop Heber in Northern India* (Cambridge: Cambridge University Press, 1971), p. 2.

317. R.C. Majumdar (ed.), *British Paramountcy and Indian Renaissance* (Bombay: Bharatiya Vidya Bhavan, 1965), Part II, p. 274.

318. Dilip Kumar Biswas and Prabhat Chandra Ganguli (eds.), Sophia Dobson Collet: *The Life and Letters of Raja Rammohun Roy* (Calcutta: Sadharan Brahmo Samaj, 1962), pp. 255-257.

319. Alan Bouquet, *Hinduism* (London: Hutchinson, 1948), p. 32. Some doubts have been expressed as to how well-known and authoritative the Gita was in the early decades of the nineteenth century. Charles Wilkin's translation and preface (Hendrik; p. 2) seems to testify to its popularity, so also Roy, who even refers to it as a work "whose authority is considered most sacred by Hindus of all persuasions". The fact, however, that the Gītā is a *smṛti* and not a *śruti* text should not be lost sight of.

320. Agehananda Bharati, "The Hindu Renaissance, Its Apologetic Pattern" *Journal of Asian Studies*, 29 (2) 267-287. Lewis Sydney Stewart O'Malley (ed.), *Modern India and the West* (London: Oxford University Press, 1968), p. 230. Gerald James Larson, "The Bhagavadgita as crosscultural process: Towards an analysis of the social location of a religious text", *Journal of the American Academy of Religion* 43 (4) 651-669.

321. These citations are: II.40.42-44.49; III.9.26ab; V.12; VI.41; IX. 21.32; X.32c; XII.10-11 and XVIII.6.

322. Pandurang Vaman Kane, *History of Dharmaśāstra* (Poona: Bhandarkar Oriental Research Institute, 1941), Vol. II, p. 631.

323. T.M.P. Mahadevan, *Outlines of Hinduism* (Bombay: Chetana, 1971), p. 86; M. Hiriyanna, *Essentials of Indian Philosophy* (London: George Allen & Unwin, 1949), p. 54.

324. Rammohun Roy, *Translation of a Conference Between an Advocate for and an Opponent of, the Practice of Burning Widows Alive from the Original Bungla* (Calcutta: Rammohun Roy, 1818), p. 111.

325. Rammohun Roy, *Translation of an Abridgement of the Vadant* (Calcutta: Rammohun Roy, 1818), p. 117.

326. The only scholar I know of who does not accept this interpretation is Bhāskara (Singer, 1966: 32).

327. Rammohun Roy, *Translation of a Conference...*, p. 111; T.M.P. Mahadevan, *op. cit.*, p. 136.

328. Rammohun Roy, *Translation of a Conference...*, p. 111.

329. *Ibid.*, p. 112.

330. T.M.P. Mahadevan, *op. cit.*, p. 139.

331. Rammohun Roy, *Translation of a Conference...*, p. 112.

332. *Ibid.*, p. 106. Eric J. Sharpe thus situates Roy's use of the Gītā in the broader context of its role in the modern period of Indian history (*The Universal Gita* [London: Duckworth, 1985] pp. 13-14): "On this occasion Roy was speaking, not to the masses, but to those in whose hands the everyday conduct of Hindu affairs still lay—the brahmins on the one hand and the British administrators on the other (the 'Conference' was first published in Bengali

and subsequently translated into English). In India in 1820 the machinery of popular education had hardly begun to be set up; literacy was uncommon; the Gita though fully accessible and supremely authoritative to 'the learned', was not yet a 'popular' writing, nor had it begun to be coupled with the political process. Its *Sitz im Leben* was within the intricacies of *dharma* in all its aspects, day-to-day practices as well as ultimate goals. Arvind Sharma has argued that on this occasion the Gita played an important role in the abolition of Sati, alongside the social and political forces which have been more commonly acknowledged. In this he is surely right. Roy's 1820 argument was founded on the Gita's doctrine of 'desireless action', and the Gita thus made, it might be argued, its first entry into the field of modern Indian politics. Over half a century was to elapse, however, before it assumed a dominant role in that volatile area."

333. H. Spiegelberg. *The Phenomenological Movement: A Historical Introduction.* Vol. II. (The Hague: Martinus Nijhoff, 1965), p. 657.

334. Eric J. Sharpe. *Comparative Religion: A History* (London: Gerald Duckworth and Co., 1975), p. 237.

335. For example, Abbe J.A. Dubois in his *Hindu Manners, Customs and Ceremonies* (Oxford: Clarendon Press, 1959), pp. 355-66, refers to sati as a "barbarous custom", the women as "victims of this horrid superstition" or "wretched fanatics". He opines: "But think of the numberless young widows in the prime of life and strength. How do they bear up against this cruel expulsion from the society of their fellow creatures?", p. 354.

336. The time frame for the present paper is between the 10th and the 19th centuries when sati became fully entrenched in Hindu ideology. The Dharmaśāstras explicitly forbid the killing of a woman on any account. See P.V. Kane, *History of Dharmaśāstra* Vol. II, Part I (Poona: Bhandarkar Oriental Institute, 1974), p. 575; hereafter referred to as Kane, Vol. II (Part I or II). Also Kane states: "*Sati* was not in historic times a practice imposed by priests or men on unwilling women...It may be that examples of *sati* occurred because of the force of popular sentiment" (p. 630). Similarly Kane concludes that the Dharmaśāstras generally condemn suicide as a great sin (Vol. II, Part II, p. 924 ff.). The death rituals were not to be performed for a person who committed suicide. Thus we see that sati was not viewed as a homicide or suicide by Hindus, though it did come under the larger category of religious self-willed death.

337. A woman had the option whether to perform sati or to undergo the rite of passage to widowhood. Every precaution was to be taken that the sati knew what she was doing and had the strength to endure the consequences of her resolve (*saṁkalpa*). For example, her relatives would vigorously try to dissuade her and the priests would test her strength. See note 349. Thus only if there was overt pressure by family or priests prior to her resolve could sati be called homicide, according to the tradition. We conclude that any action that influenced directly a woman's decision so that it was not her own resolve was adharmic. Such adharmic attempts to influence a woman's decision have been recorded and no doubt became more numerous as the custom of sati became more common. Kane notes that in Bengal where sati was most popular, families may have exploited this custom as a way to eliminate the widow,who had the

right to her husband's property until her death. See Kane, Vol. II, Part I, p. 635.

338. *Vidhavā* is a Sanskrit word with the following etymology given by Hindu grammarians: *vigataḥ dhavaḥ yasyāḥ sā*, the one whose husband is gone, i.e. is dead, therefore a widow.

See Kane, Vol. II, Part, I, pp. 583-623 for a discussion of *śruti* and *smṛti* texts that refer to the term *vidhavā*, the duties of a widow, the tonsure of a widow and the issues of remarriage and divorce.

339. The adjective *tapasvin* means distressed, wretched, poor, miserable; it also means the one who practises austerities. In its feminine form it means a female devotee or a poor, wretched woman. *Tapasvin* comes from the noun *tapas*, which is derived from the verbal root *tap* which means to give out heat, to suffer pain, to practise austerity (*tapas*), to undergo penance. See Sir Monier Williams, *A Sanskrit-English Dictionary* (Oxford: Clarendon Press, 1970), pp. 436-437; hereafter referred to as Monier-Williams.

340. The word *satī* is a present participle in feminine form (from the verbal root *as* to be), which means a woman who truly exists, therefore a perfect female being. It is also a feminine form of the adjective *sat* (a present participle, from *as*) which means good, therefore a good woman.

341. *Śubha* means auspicious; *aśubha* means not simply the lack of auspiciousness but positive evil. (The prefix *a* implies not merely absence of something, but rather the emphatic opposite.)

342. In colloquial Marāṭhī, the words synonymous with ogress or witch are used for a widow, especially the long-living one (*melīne navryālā khālle anī āpaṇ saglyānmā khāun baslī āhe*: the cursed woman has eaten up her husband and having eaten up almost everyone else, she is living comfortably). The words for witch (*ceṭakī*) or vampire, human-devouring ogress (*lavsat*) are also used in vulgar speech. These words convey an emotional effect but not an ontic effect, i.e. a *lavsat* or vampire refers to a being in the interim period between death and the next birth. Therefore, cursing the widow as *lavsat* cannot ontically change her into a vampire, but it can emotionally castigate her.

343. For an analysis of the concept of *tilaka* see Katherine Young's "The Beguiling Simplicity of a Dot" in *Arc* Vol. VI no. 2, Spring, 1979, published by the Faculty of Religious Studies, McGill University.

344. The entrance into widowhood is a *rite de passage*. Abbe J.A. Dubois (*op. cit.*, p. 353) gives an account: "A very few days after the death of her husband, a widow's house is invaded by female friends and relatives, who begin by eating a meal prepared for them. After this they surround the widow and exhort her to bear her miserable lot with fortitude. One after another they take her in their arms, shed tears with her, and end by pushing her violently to the ground. They next join together in lamenting her widowhood, and finally make her sit on a small stool. Then, one of her nearest female relatives, having previously muttered some religious formulae, cuts the thread of the *tali*, the gold ornament which every married woman in India wears around her neck. The barber is called in, and her head is clean shaved. This double ceremony sinks her instantly into the despised and hated class of widows. During the whole time that these curious and mournful rites are being performed, the unfortunate victim is making the

whole house resound with her cries of woe, cursing her sad lot a thousand times."

345. *Dharma* is that which is established, practice, duty, justice, virtue, morality, religion, religious merit, good works. See Monier-Williams, p. 510.

346. *Adharma* is not simply the absence of *dharma* but rather positive evil, immorality, religious demerit (*pāpa*), injustice.

347. See Kane, Voll II, Part I, pp. 624-636 for the textual references on the practice of sati.

348. "Perform" is a semantically unmarked verb connoting simply the sense of "do", whereas "commit" is associated with words that convey acts of negative connotation. "Perform" is also used with positively "marked" semantics in the sense of "doing a good deed".

349. "At some places, if the sati did not want to abandon her resolution, her level of endurance was tested. In this test certain things were detected, e.g. can the woman sit on a funeral pyre and withstand until the end the unbearable procedure of the act of sati? And would she be a disgrace to the family by running away from it? For this purpose they used to test her by placing a limb of hers in the flame of a lamp. If she could bear that suffering with equanimity, then people took her as a true sati and cooperated with her in fulfilling her resolve." See Shivasahayaji Caturvedi, *Satīdāha* (Allahabad: Chand Karyalaya, 1926), pp. 107-108. This is a Hindi translation of the original Bengali work by Kumudanath Mallik (hereafter referred to as *Satīdāha*). The excerpts in this paper from *Satīdāha* are translations from Hindi into English by Alaka Hegib.

If a sati did not follow through on sati, it was thought that the whole town would face a disaster. *Satīdāha*, p. 126.

350. The Dharmaśāstras prescribe penances for a woman who turns away from the act of sati after having made her resolve (*saṁkalpa*) for the act. See Kane, Vol. II, Part I, p. 633. "After examination of historical case studies, it is known that when a woman expressed her desire to perform sati, her sons, daughters, and close, concerned relatives tried to dissuade her from that act and sometimes they were successful." *Satīdāha*, pp. 107-108. According to *Satīdāha*, p. 159, sati was prohibited for pregnant women and women with small children.

351. Sati was also performed at the confluence of rivers, any river, tank, or any place of water. Because any *tīrtha* (literally a place of water, tank; conventionally a holy place) was an auspicious place, it was a suitable locus for the auspicious act of sati. When the husband was cremated elsewhere or his corpse was lost, and the wife learned of his death, she would be burnt along with his ashes or his sandals. This type of sati, termed *anumaraṇa*, often occurred at the above mentioned places.

352. The sati not only conferred auspiciousness on her family and the witnesses of the event, she also contributed positively to the prosperity of the kingdom. The transference of the sati's auspiciousness, which is like a magical power, occurred in several other situations. The *Satīdāha* (p. 126) mentions that it was believed that the belongings of a sati contained healing power and so through touch of them a cure could occur. Because a sati is a married woman par ex-

cellence, her *sindur* (red powder from the parting of her hair) was considered potent. It was believed that if one "Puts the *sindur* of a sati in the hair of a woman to be married, it overcomes fear or indifference to the first sexual act.", p. 126. Here we find the transference associated not with the general semantics of *śubha* as auspiciousness, prosperity, well-being but rather the particular semantics of fertility, especially a woman's fertility. As the number of satis increased, however, there seems to have been some misgivings. We are told in *Satīdāha* (p. 126) that "People used to believe that the year in which and the kingdom in which there were too many satis, there was some disaster in store for that king and that kingdom that year."

353. See James Haughton Woods, trans., *The Yoga-System of Patañjali* (Delhi: Motilal Banarsidass, 1966), pp. 30-32.

354. The authors of the Dharmaśāstras occasionally view the widow and the ascetic as one category: e.g. Kane, Vol. II, Part I, p. 484: "Pracetas forbids to an ascetic and a widow the chewing of betel leaves, ceremonial bath...and taking meal in a vessel of bellmetal."
Kane himself recognizes the parallelism of imagery between the widow and the ascetic: "She had not only to lead a life of perfect celibacy...but she had to act like an ascetic, being poorly fed (only once a day) and poorly clad" p. 586. Also, "As widows were equated with *yatis* for several injunctions...and as the latter shaved themselves, widows were gradually required to do so", p. 592. Kane also points to the tonsure of Buddhist and Jaina nuns as models for this practice, p. 592. Even the practice of the widow's wearing reddish-colored saris in regions such as Maharashtra may be considered a parallel to the ochre robes of the monks and nuns. See Kane, p. 593.

355. *Yoga* is a universal feature of Indian culture. *Yoga* can be applied to any realm of life given certain presuppositions that are essential to the standard *yogas*. *Yoga* is both *upāya* and *upeya*. As *upāya*, *yoga* is a methodology: anything that cultivates the sustenance and rigor that is necessary to attain the goal. As *upeya*, it is the message. Adequately applied, the method is converted into a *darśana* (view, philosophy). Therefore, every *yoga* has the elements of a *darśana*; this is true conversely. In the woman's context, this universal *yoga* has also been applied; her life is also disciplined to cultivate the sustenance and rigor to attain her goal; she has her own view (*darśana*) by which she realizes her supreme goal. Hence we may coin another term and speak of *strīyoga*, the discipline and goal for a woman, which pervades her life in its various stages as maiden, wife (and widow or sati should the husband die first). The woman's *yoga* provides both self-control and self-denial and helps her to attain (and maintain) the goal: union with the husband.

356. For an analysis of the religious and historical factors that caused women in general to be rebirth rather than *mokṣa* oriented see Katherine Young, "Why are Hindu Women Traditionally Oriented to Rebirth Rather than Liberation (*moksa*)?" in *Third International Symposium on Asian Studies* (Hong Kong: Asian Research Service), pp. 937-945.

357. "According to the *śāstras* a woman who makes a voluntary resolve to perform sati was not considered a widow. Hence she used to be beautifully bedecked like a fortunate married woman (*sadhavā*), putting the *sindūr* (red powder)

in the parting of her hair. Riding in...a palanquin, she used to follow the funeral procession of the husband toward the cremation ground" (*Satīdāha*, p. 117).

358. *Satīśiromaṇi*: sati, the crest-jewel: "In those days people used to believe that the woman who, upon overhearing the talk of her husband's death, drops dead before even touching the funeral pyre, is the crest-jewel, and she is worshipped in heaven" (*Satīdāha*, p. 111).

359. In this sense the sati may be compared to the *bodhisattva* who generates an excess of merit by his self-sacrifice including the giving of his life, and can transfer this merit to others.

360. Kane, Vol. II, Part I, pp. 583-4 cites some passages from the Dharmaśāstras which claim that if a virtuous woman after the death of her husband abides by the rule of celibacy, engages in religious observances and fasts, and restrains her senses, she will go to heaven.
Whereas the texts on sati almost always hold out the promise of heaven, those on the *vidhavā* do so only occasionally. We conclude that the widow lived with ambiguity regarding her destiny.

361. The promise of heaven was associated with death caused by entering fire. "In the Rāmāyaṇa (Araṇya, Chap. 9) Śarabhaṅga is said to have entered fire. The Mṛcchakaṭika (1:4) speaks of King Śūdraka who entered fire. In Gupta Inscription No. 42, the great Emperor Kumāragupta is said to have entered the fire of dried cowdung cakes" (Kane, Vol. II, Part II, p. 927). "In Bengal, Bihar, and Orissa, there was a custom of burying women alive with the deceased husband. This custom was prevalent in the communities of Jogi, Jola, and Vaiṣṇava" (*Satīdāha*, p. 122).

362. *Bhaktiyoga* encompasses a number of different views. While in earlier forms of *yoga*, a *yogī* meditated on god as *a means* to develop single-pointed attention, in *bhaktiyoga* a *yogī* focused on God as the *Supreme Reality*. *Bhaktiyoga* was also open to householders including women. Thus a woman could continue to observe her *strīdharma* with her attention on her husband but also direct her attention to God. The attainment of Heaven would presumably satisfy both her goals of reunion with the husband and union with God, though we have not seen this point spelled out as such. In that *bhaktiyoga* also encompassed love and service it is understandable why a woman internalized this religious orientation in her observance of *strīdharma*.

363. The *Satīdāha*, pp. 106-107, illustrates the psychological complexity surrounding sati. We are told that "women used to be attracted to the act of sati for the following reasons:

1. Deep love for the husband.
2. Veda, Purāṇa, Śāstra, and Smṛtis have extolled the greatness of a sati, and women believe in this.
3. The desire to enjoy pleasures for 30,000 years upon freeing the husband through the act of sati from all *pāpas*.
4. The hope of attaining infinite pleasures upon momentary agony of being burnt by the fire of the funeral pyre.
5. A relief from harsh suffering on account of the deprivation of sex in widowhood.

6. Aspiration for renown, i.e. inclusion in the list of the good satis whose names are chanted as a form of morning worship.
7. The common belief of Hindus that life is transient and therefore detachment toward life should be cultivated.

To those women who volunteer to perform sati after the death of their husband, the following thoughts and anxieties occur:

1. It is futile for a woman to continue mundane existence after the husband is dead.
2. The love for children can never match the love for the husband.
3. Now she must be a refugee in the same household in which she had been a mistress concerning every last detail. As a refugee she is bound to go through the sufferings of widowhood, and finally to die.
4. It is better to be peaceful forever after momentary endurance of the flames than remain a wretched widow for many years. After all, everyone has to face death someday. So why miss the auspicious occasion of obtaining heaven by following this way (performing sati)? Many good women of the past like us have offered up their lives in the funeral pyre on such occasions. So why should we fear?

This is the psychology of women who volunteered to perform sati."

BIBLIOGRAPHY

Altekar, A.S. *The Position of Women in Hindu Civilization.* Delhi, Motilal Banarsidass, 1962; 1963; Patna, Motilal Banarsidass, 1973.

Avineri, Shlomo. *Karl Marx on Colonialism and Modernisation.* New York, Anchor Books, 1969.

Aziz, Ahmad. *Studies in Islamic Culture in the Indian Environment.* Oxford, Clarendon Press, 1964.

Ball, Upendra Nath. *Rammohun Roy.* Calcutta, U. Ray & Sons, 1933.

Basham, A.L. *The Wonder That Was India.* New York, Grove Press Inc., 1959.

Basu, Major P.D. *Rise of the Christian Power in India.* Vol. IV. Calcutta, R. Chatterjee, 1925.

Bengal : Past and Present, Vol. 94, Pt. 2, No. 179, July/Dec. 1975.

Bharati, Agehananda. "The Hindu Renaissance, Its Apologetic Pattern", in *Journal of Asian Studies,* 29:2, 1970.

Bhattacharya, Sachchidananda. *A Dictionary of Indian History.* New York, George Brazilier, 1937.

Biswas, Dilip Kumar and Prabhat Chandra Ganguli (eds.). Sophia Dobson Collet, *The Life and letters of Raja Rammohun Roy.* Calcutta, Sadharana Brahmo Samaj, 1962.

Blackham, R.J. *Incomparable India.* London, Sampson Low, 1935.

Bouquet, Alan. *Hinduism.* London, Hutchinson, 1948.

Brailsford, Henry Noel. *Subject India.* New York, John Day Co., 1943.

Brown, W. Norman. *The United States and India and Pakistan.* Harvard University Press, 1963.

Buchanan, Claudius. "The Star in the East with Three New Sermons"; and "Memoir of the Expediency of an Ecclesiastical Establishment for British India", in *The Works of the Rev. Claudius Buchanan.* New York, 1812.

Calcott, Maria (Dundas) Graham. *Letters on India.* London, 1814.

Calcutta Gazette, Mon. 27 June 1831 and 18 January 1930.

Calcutta Journal, 20 January 1820.

Carey, Eustace. *Memoirs of William Carey.* London, Jackson & Walford, 1836.

Carey, S. Pearce. *William Carey* (5th Edn). London, 1924.

Caturvedi, Shivasahayaji. *Satīdāha.* Allahabad, Chand Karyalaya, 1926.

Chaudhury, Sushil. "A Note on 'Sati' in Medieval India", in *Indian Historical Congress Proceedings* 1964 (Aligarh, Indian Historical Congress, 1967) Part II, Section II.

Chirol, Valentine. *Indian Unrest.* London, Macmillan & Co., 1910.

Collet, Sophia Dobson. *The Life and Letters of Raja Rammohun Roy.* Calcutta, Sadharan Brahma Samaj, 1962.

Coomaraswamy, Ananda K. *The Dance of Shiva.* New York, Noonday Press, 1957.

———. "Sati: A Defense of the Indian Woman", in *The Sociological Review,* April 1913.

Coupland, R. *India: A Restatement.* London, Oxford University Press, 1945.

Cowell, E.B. and F.W. Thomas (Trans). *The Harṣacarita of Bāṇa.* London, Royal Asiatic Society, 1897.

Crooke, William (ed.). Sir H. Yule and A.C. Burnell's, *Hobson-Jobson.* Delhi, Munshiram Manoharlal, 1968.

Datta, V.N. *Sati: A Historical, Social and Philosophical Enquiry into the Hindu Rite of Widow Burning.* New Delhi, Manohar Books, 1988.

Dodwell, H.H. (ed.). *The Cambridge History of India,* Vol. VI. Cambridge University Press, 1932; and Delhi, S. Chand & Co., 1964.

Dubois, Abbe J.A. *Hindu Manners, Customs and Ceremonies.* Oxford, Clarendon Press, 1947; 1959.

Durant, Will. *The Case for India.* New York, Simon and Schuster, 1930.

Edwards, Michael, *British India.* New York, Hawthorn Books, 1963; New York, Taplinger Publishing Co., 1967.

Embree, A.T. *Charles Grant and British Rule in India.* New York, Columbia University Press, 1963.

Encyclopedia Britannica, Vol. 15; Vol. 21. London, William Benton, 1968.

Essays Relative to the Habits, Characters and Moral Improvement of the Hindoos. London, Kingsbury, Parbury & Allen, 1823.

Extract Judicial Consultations, 7 February 1805, in *G.B. Parliament: Papers Relating to East India Affairs,* viz., Hindoo Widows and Voluntary Immolation, Vol. I.

Farquhar, J.N. *The Crown of Hinduism.* London, Oxford University Press, 1913.

———. *Modern Religious Movements in India.* Delhi, Munshiram Manoharlal, 1967.

Field, Harry H. *After Mother India.* New York, Harcourt Brace & Co., 1929.

Frazer, R.W. *British India.* New York, G.P. Putnam's Sons, 1918.

Friend of India, October 1819.

Fuller, Mrs Marcus B. *The Wrongs of Indian Womanhood.* New York, Young People's Missionary Movement, 1900.

Garratt, G.T. *An Indian Commentary.* London, Jonathon Cape, n.d.

G.B. Parliament, House of Commons Debates, Vol. 26, 22 June 1813.

Gopal, Ram, *British Rule in India.* London, Asia Publishing House, 1963.

———. *Lokamanya Tilak.* New Delhi, Asia Publishing House, 1956.

Griffiths, Sir Percival, *The British Impact on India.* London, Cass, 1965.

Heber, Reginald. *Narrative of a Journey Through the Upper Provinces of India.* London, 1961.

Hiriyanna, M. *Essentials of Indian Philosophy.* London, George Allen & Unwin, 1949.

Indra. *The Status of Women in Ancient India.* Delhi, Motilal Banarsidass, 1955.

Ingham, Kenneth. *Reformers* in *India,* 1793-1833. Cambridge University Press, 1956.

Jha, Mahamahopadhyaya Ganganath. *Manu Smriti.* University of Calcutta, 1926.

Johns, William. *A Collection of Facts and Opinions Relative to the Burning of Widows with the Dead Bodies of their Husbands.* Birmingham, W.H. Pearce, 1816.

Kane, P.V. (ed.). *The Harshacharita of Bāṇabhaṭṭa.* Bombay, 1918.

———. *History of Dharmaśāstra,* Poona, Bhandarkar Oriental Research Institute, 1941-1974.

Karmarkar, D.P. *Bal Gangadhar Tilak.* Bombay, Popular Book Dept., 1956.

Karve, Irawati. *Hindu Society-An Interpretation.* Poona, Deccan College, 1861.

Kavanagh Boulger, Demetrius Charles de. *Lord William Bentinck.* Oxford, Clarendon Press, 1892.

Laird, M.A. (ed.). *Bishop Heberr in Northern India.* Cambridge University Press, 1972.

Lanman, Charles Rockwell. *A Sanskrit Reader.* Harvard University Press, 1971.

Larson, Gerald James. "The Bhagavadgita as cross-cultural process: towards an analysis of the social location of a religious text", in *Journal of the American Academy of Religion,* 43; 4, 1975.

Macdonell, A.A. *A History of Sanskrit Literature.* London, William Heinemann, 1913.

———. *The Vedic Mythology.* Varanasi, Indological Bookhouse, 1971.

Macmunn, Sir George. *The Religions and Hidden Cults of India.* London, Sampson Low, 1931.

Mahadevan, T.M.P., *Outlines of Hinduism.* Bombay, Chetana Ltd, 1960; 1971.

Mahfuz-ul-haq, M. (ed.). *Majna-ul-Bahrain.* Calcutta, Asiatic Society of Bengal, 1929.

Maitra, Harendranath. *Hinduism: The World Ideal.* New York, Dodd, Mead & Co. 1916.

Majumdar, R.C. (ed.). *The Age of Imperial Unity.* Bombay, Bharatiya Vidya Bhavan. 1953.

———. *The Struggle for Empire.* Bombay, Bharatiya Vidya Bhavan, 1966.

———. *British Paramountcy and Indian Renaissance,* Vol. I. Bombay, Bharatiya Vidya Bhavan, 1963; Vol. II, Bombay, Bharatiya Vidya Bhavan, 1965.

Majumdar, R.C., H.C. Raychaudhuri and Kalikinkar Datta. *An Advanced History of India.* London, Macmillan & Co., 1948; London, St Martin's Street, 1950; New York, St Martin's Press, 1967.

Marshall, P.J. (ed.). *The British Discovery of Hinduism in the Eighteenth Century.* Cambridge University Press, 1970.

Marshman, John Clark. *The Life and Times of Carey, Marshman and Ward.* London, 1859.

Mayo, Katherine. *Mother India.* New York, Blue Ribbon Books, 1927.

Mill, James. *The History of British India.* New York, Chelsea House Publishers, 1968.

Missionary Register, 1820; 1821.

Monier-Williams, Sir Monier. *Indian Wisdom.* London, H. Allen & Co., 1875.

———. *A Sanskrit-English Dictionary.* Oxford, Clarendon Press, 1970.

Muir, Peter. *This Is India.* New York, Doubleday, Doran & Co., 1943.

Muir, Ramsay. *The Making of British India:* 1756-1858. Manchester University Press, 1915.

Murty, K. Satchidananda, *Revelation and Reason in Advaita Vedānta.* New York, Columbia University Press, 1959.

Nandargikar, C.B. *The Raghuvaṁśa of Kālidāsa.* Bombay, Radhabhai Atmaran Sagoon, 1897.

Nehru, Jawaharlal. *The Discovery of India.* New York, John Day, 1946.

New Standard Dictionary of the English Language. New York, Funk & Wagnall's Co., 1951.

O'Malley, Lewis Sydney Stewart (ed.). *Modern India and the West.* London, Oxford University Press, 1968.

Pandey, B.N. *The Break-up of the British Empire.* New York, St Martin's Press, 1969.

Panikkar, K.M. *Hindu Society at the Cross Roads.* Bombay, Asia Publishing House, 1955.

Parkes, Fanny. *Wanderings of a Pilgrim in Search of the Picturesque,* Vol. I. London, 1850.

Parvate, T.V. *Bal Gangadhar Tilak.* Ahmedabad, Navajivan Publishing House, 1958.

Pegg, James. *The Suttee's Cry to Britain.* London, Sealy & Son, 1827.

———. *India's Cries to British Humanity* (2nd Edn.). London, 1830.

Penzer, N.M. (ed.). *The Ocean of Story,* Vol. IV. London, Charles J. Sawyer, 1925.

Philips, C.M. (ed.). *Historians of India, Pakistan and Ceylon.* Oxford, Clarendon Press, 1961.

———. *The Correspondence of Lord William Cavendish Bentinck.* Oxford, Clarendon Press, 1977.

Pinkham, M.W. *Woman in the Sacred Scriptures of Hinduism.* New York, Columbia University Press, 1941.

Powell-Price, J.C. *A History of India.* New York, Thomas Nelson & Sons Ltd., 1955.

Prasad, Ram Chandra. *Early English Travellers in India.* Delhi, Motilal Banarsidass, 1965.

Regulation XVII of 1829.

Renou, Louis. *The Nature of Hinduism.* New York, Walker & Company, 1964.

Riencourt, Amaury de. *The Soul of India.* New York, Harper Brothers, 1960.

Roberto, P.E. *History of British India.* Oxford, Clarendon Press, 1923.

Roy, Rammohun. *The Practice of Burning Widows Alive* (advertisement). Calcutta, 1818.

———. *Translation of an Abridgement of the Vedant.* Calcutta, 1818.

———. *Translation of a Conference Between an Advocate for and an Opponent of the Practice of Burning Widows Alive from the Original Bungla.* Calcutta, 1818.

———. *The English Works of Raja Rammohun Roy,* Part 4. Calcutta, 1947.

Sambada Bhaskara, 26 May 1849.

Sastri, P.P.S. (ed.). *The Mahabharata,* Vol. I, Pt. 1. Madras, V. Ramaswamy Sastrulu Sons, 1931.

Sastry, N. Yagnesvara. *Stri-Dharma,* July 1928.

Sati, *Seminar* issue 342, February 1988

Sen, Surendra Nath. *Eighteen Fifty Seven.* New Delhi, Government of India, Publications Division, 1957.

Sewell, Robert. *A Forgotten Empire.* London, Swan Sonnenschein, 1900.

Sharma, Neeta. *Bāṇabhaṭṭa: A Literary Study.* Delhi, Munshiram Monoharlal, 1968.

Sharpe, Enc. J. *Comparative Religion: A History.* London, Gerald Duckworth Co., 1975.

———. *The Universal Gita.* London, Duckworth, 1985.

Shay, Theodore L. *The Legacy of the Lokamanya.* Oxford, Clarendon Press, 1956.

Shore, Frederick John. *Notes on Indian Affairs.* London, 1837.

Singh, Iqbal. *Rammohun Roy.* Vol. I. New Delhi, Asia Publishing House, 1958.

Singer, Milton (ed.). *Krishna: Myths, Rites, Attitudes.* Honolulu, East-West Center Press, 1966.

Singhal, D.P. *Nationalism in India and Other Historical Essays.* Delhi, Munshiram Manoharlal, 1967.

Sleeman, W.H. *Rambles and Recollections of an Indian Official.* London, 1915 (revised ed.).

Smith, George, *The Life of William Carey.* London, John Murray, 1885.

Smith, Vincent A. *The Oxford History of India.* Oxford, Clarendon Press, 1919.

Spear, Percival. *India.* Ann Arbor, University of Michigan Press, 1961.

Spear, Percival (ed.). *The Oxford History of India.* Oxford, Clarendon Press, 1967, 1985.

Spiegelberg, H. *The Phenomenological Movement: A Historical Introduction,* Vol. II. The Hague, Martinus Nijoff, 1965.

Spratt, P. *Hindu Culture and Personality.* Bombay, Manaktalas, 1966.

Srinivas, M.N. *Religion and Society Among the Coorgs of South India.* Oxford, Clarendon Press, 1952.

———. *Caste in Modern India.* New Delhi, Asia Publishing House, 1962.

Tahmankar, D.V. *Lokamanya Tilak.* London, John Murray, 1956.

Tawney, C.H. (Trans.). *The Ocean of Story,* Vol. 4, App. 1. London, 1924.

Thomas, P. *Indian Women Through the Ages.* London, Asia Publishing House, 1964.

Thompson, Edward. *Suttee.* London, George Allen & Unwin, 1928.

Tinker, Hugh. *India and Pakistan.* New York, F.A. Praeger, 1962.

Tylor, Edward B. *Primitive Culture,* Vol. 1, Boston, Estes & Lauriat, 1874.

Upadhyaya, Bhagwat Saran. *Women in Rgveda.* Benares, Nand Kishore & Bros, 1941.

van Buitenen, J.A.B. *The Mahabharata,* Vol. I, University of Chicago Press, 1973.

Vivekananda, Swami. *The Complete Works of..,* Vol. III, Calcutta, Advaita Ashram, 1960; Vol. IV, Calcutta, Advaita Ashram, 1955.

Walker, Benjamin. *The Hindu World,* Vol. II. New York, Frederick A. Praeger, 1968.

Walker, F. Deaville. *William Carey.* Chicago, Moody Press, 1951.

Ward, William. *Necessity of Christianity to India.* Boston, 1 Jan. 1821.

Ward, Rev. William. *A View of the History, Literature and Religion of the Hindus.* London, 1817; Hartford, H. Huntingdon, 1824.

Webster's Third New International Dictionary. Springfield, Mass., G. & C. Merrian & Co., 1959.

Whitney, William Dwight. *Artharva-Veda-Samhita*, Vol. II. Delhi, Motilal Banarsidass, 1971.

Wilkins, W.J. *Modern Hinduism*. London, T. Fisher Unwin, 1887.

Williams, Raymond Brady. *A New Face of Hindusm: The Swaminarayan Religion*. Cambridge University Press, 1984.

Wolpert, Stanley A. *Tilak and Gokhale: Revolution and Reform in the Making of Modern India*. University of California Press, 1962.

Woodruff, Philip. *The Men Who Ruled India*, Vol. I, London, Jonathon Cape, 1953; Vol. II, New York, St Martin's Press, 1954.

Woods, James Haughton (trans.). *The Yoga System of Patanjali*. Delhi, Motilal Banarsidass, 1966.

Young, Katherine. "The Beguiling Simplicity of Dot", in *Arc*, Vol. VI, No. 2, Spring 1979.

———. "Why Are Hindu Women Traditionally Oriented to Rebirth Rather than Liberation (moksa)?" in *Third International Symposium on Asian Studies*, Hong Kong, Asian Research Service, 1981.

Zaehner, R.C. *Hinduism*. Oxford, Clarendon Press, 1962.

SANSKRIT INDEX

Adharma 16, 76, 110 (n. 346)
Āgama 17
Agneḥ 35, 102 (n. 211)
Aṅgiras 31, 51
Antyeṣṭi 81
Anugamana 39, 86 (n. 10)
Anumaraṇa 32, 39, 86 (n. 10), 101 (n. 195), 102 (n. 206), 103 (n. 223), 110 (n. 351)
Anuvāka 37, 103 (n. 215)
Anvārohaṇa 16, 32, 39, 101 (n. 185)
Āpad-Dharma 102 (n. 206)
Aparigraha 79
Arthavāda 35, 36, 37
Aśāstrīya 16
Aśubha 75, 82, 109 (n. 341)
Āsvalāyana 102 (n. 211)
Aukhya Śākhā 37, 103 (n. 215)

Baudhāyana-Pitṛmedha-Sūtra 34
Bhagavadgītā (also see Gītā) 52, 67, 69, 107 (n. 319)
Bhāgavata Purāṇa 32
Bhaktiyoga 83, 112 (n. 362)
Bhoga 75
Bodhisattva 112 (n. 359)
Brahmacarya 16, 78, 79
Brāhmaṇa/s 16, 25, 26, 27, 29, 30, 32, 33, 100 (n. 181), 102 (n. 211), 108 (n. 219)
Brahmans 9, 20
Brahmapurāṇa 31, 102 (n. 211)
Brahmarṣi 33
Brahmins x, 26, 57, 58, 60
Bṛhaddevatā 34
Brhan-Nāradīya Purāṇa 32
Bṛhaspati 32, 51

Caṇḍāla 32
Ceṭakī 109 (n. 342)

Darśana 111 (n. 355)
Dāyabhāga xi, 5
Dharma 16, 37, 76, 77, 102 (n. 206), 110 (n. 345)
Dharma Sabhā 62
Dharma Śāstras 108 (n. 336), 110 (n. 350), 111 (n. 354)
Dharmasūtras 22, 92-93 (n. 82), 101 (n. 193)

Ekāgratā 79

Gautamīmāhātmya 31
Gītā—see Bhagavadgītā 67, 69, 70, 71
Gṛhasthāśrama 79
Gṛhyasūtra 102 (n. 211)

Harśacarita 39

Jīvaloka 37

Kādambarī 15
Kapotī 33
Karma (Karman) 70, 76, 78, 80, 81, 84, 101 (n. 193)
Karmayoga 70
Kena Upaniṣad 52
Kṛṣṇa (Krishna) 32, 33, 64
Kṣatriyas (Kshatriyas) x, 29
Kumārsambhava 103 (n. 229)

Madanapārijāta 32
Mahābhārata 25, 26, 33, 87 (n. 11), 101-102 (n. 204)
Mahānirvāṇa Tantra 16
Mahāparinirvāṇatantra 17
Mahāprasthāna 82
Manu, Manusmṛti, Manusaṁhitā, Mānava-Dharma-Śāstra 22, 33, 52, 67, 89 (n. 52), 93-94 (n. 94), 97-98 (n. 118), 102 (n. 205, 206)
Mausala-Parva 33
Mitākṣarā 32, 98 (n. 128), 101 (n. 185)
Mokṣa 97, 82, 111-112 (n. 356)
Mṛcchakaṭika 112 (n. 361)
Muṇḍaka Upaniṣad 52

Nārāyaṇīya Taittirīya Upaniṣad 103 (n. 215)
Narāyanīya Upaniṣad (Upanishad) 37, 103 (n. 215)
Ni-Pad
Niṣkāma Karma 67
Niyama 78
Niyoga 34

Padmapurāṇa 29, 101-102 (n. 204)
Pādukā 103 (n. 223)
Pāpa 110 (n. 346), 112-113 (n. 363)
Paramparā 77
Parāśara (Parāshara; Parāśarasaṁhitā) 30, 31, 101 (n. 195), 101-102 (n. 204), 102 (n. 206)

Pati 83
Patideva 77
Patiyoga 80
Prājāpatya 32
Praṇāmāñjali 76
Puṇya 77, 82
Purāṇa 112-113 (n. 363)
Pūrva-Mīmāṁsā 72
Pūrvānumaraṇa 41

Raghunandana 102 (n. 211)
Raghuvaṁśa 97 (n. 113)
Rāmāyaṇa 33, 112 (n. 361)
Ṛgveda (Rigveda) 34, 35, 36, 37, 100 (n. 181), 102 (n. 211), 103 (n. 219)
Ṛgvidhāna 34

Sādhanā 78, 80
Sadhavā 112 (n. 359)
Sahagamana 15, 39, 86-87 (n. 10)
Sahamaraṇa 39, 86-87 (n. 10), 101 (n. 194)
Śākta 22
Śākta Tantras 17
Samādhi 82
Saṁkalpa 76, 84, 108-109 (n. 337), 110 (n. 350)
Saṁsāra 70
Śānti-Parva 33
Śāstras 16, 50, 52, 59, 72, 112 (n. 357), 112-113 (n. 363)
Satī 1, 39, 73, 85-86 (n. 8), 86 (n. 9), 86-87 (n. 10), 103 (n. 220), 107 (n. 315), 109 (n. 340)
Satīdāha 110 (n. 349), 110 (n. 350), 110-111 (n. 352), 112-113 (n. 363)
Satīśiromaṇi 112 (n. 358)
Satītva 77, 78
Sindūra (Sindur) 110-111 (n. 352), 112 (n. 357)
Smārta-Bhaṭṭācārya 102 (n. 211)
Smṛti (Smriti/s) ix, 15, 16, 29, 30, 31, 33, 38, 51, 67, 102 (n. 211), 107 (n. 319), 109 (n. 338), 112-113 (n. 363)
Smṛticandrikā 16
Sṛṣṭikhaṇḍa 29
Śruti 31, 34, 38, 51, 107 (n. 319), 109 (n. 338), 112 (n.362)
Strī-Dharma 77, 82
Strīparva 33
Strīyoga 105 (n. 355)
Śubha 75, 82, 104 (n. 341), 104-105 (n. 352)
Śuddhitattva 31, 101 (n. 194)
Sumaṅgalī xii
Suttee—see under Satī
Śyenayāga 16

Taittirīya Saṁhitā 37
Tantra 94-95 (n. 94)
Tāntrikas 15, 17, 22
Tap 109 (n. 339)
Tapas 33, 78, 80, 84, 109 (n. 339)
Tapasvī 83
Tapasvin 109 (n. 343)
Tapasvinī 75, 78, 83
Tilaka 75, 109 (n. 343)
Tīrtha 82, 110 (n. 351)
Tīrthayātrā 81

Upāya 79, 81, 111 (n. 355)
Upeya 79, 81, 111 (n. 355)
Uśanas 30
Uttarakāṇḍa 33
Uttara-Mīmāṁsā 72

AUTHOR INDEX

Altekar, A.S. 15, 85 (n. 6), 87 (n. 11, 16), 88 (n. 31, 33, 37-40), 90 (n.69), 92-3 (n. 82, 86), 94-95 (n. 94), 96 (n. 106), 97-98 (n. 118-8, 121-2, 126-7, 131), 99 (n. 157-8, 161), 101-102 (n. 182-3, 187-9, 191, 193-5, 204-6, 211)
Avineri, Schlomo. 93 (n. 90)
Aziz, Ahmad. 99 (n. 149)

Ball, Upendra, 99 (n. 162), 100 (n. 178), 104 (n. 241-7)
Basham, A.L. 94-5 (n. 94), 96 (n.107), 99 (n. 150)
Basu, Major P.D. 93 (n. 90-1)
Bengal: Past and Present. 105 (n. 280)
Bharati, Agehananda. 107 (n. 320)
Bhattacharya, Sachchidananda. 100 (n. 180)
Biswas, Dilip Kumar. 103 (n. 318)
Blackham, R.J. 86-87 (n. 10), 92 (n. 79)
Bouquet, Alan. 107 (n. 319)
Brailsford, Henry Noel. 94-95 (n. 94)
Brown, W. Norman. 98 (n. 135), 104 (n. 240)
Buchanan, Claudius. 57, 58, 60, 106 (n. 284-5), 106 (n. 286-7)

Calcott, Maria (Dundas) Graham. 51 (Maria Graham), 64 (Maria Graham), 106 (n. 312)
Calcutta Gazette 49, 105 (n. 274, 282)
Calcutta Journal 49, 105 (n. 265)
Carey, Eustace. 91 (n. 75)
Carey, S. Pearce. 106 (n. 288-90)
Caturvedi, Shivasahayaji. 110 (n. 349)
Chaudhury, Sushil. 100 (n. 178)
Chirol, Valentine. 92-93 (n. 82)
Collett, Sophia Dobson. 89-90 (n.54, 56, 58-9, 64-5), 91 (n. 73, 74), 93 (n. 86), 93-94 (n. 91-2), 104 (n. 242)
Coomaraswamy, Ananda K. 56, 92-3 (n. 82, 90), 96 (n. 105), 98-99 (n. 134, 137, 139, 151), 99 (n. 164-5), 104 (n. 240)
Coupland, R. 91-92 (n. 76)
Cowell, E.B. 103-104 (n. 231-2, 234-5)
Crooke, William. 85 (n. 4), 87 (n. 20), 103 (n. 221)

Datta, Kalikinkar. 87 (n. 14, 21), 88 (n. 44), 90-91 (n. 70-71), 88 (n. 43-44), 100 (n. 179), 101 (n. 191)
Dodwell, H.H. 94-95 (n. 94), 104 (n. 236, 238)
Dubois, Abbe J.A. 57, 89 (n. 51), 105 (n. 283), 108 (n. 335), 109-110 (n. 344)
Durant, Will. 91-92 (n. 76)

Edwards, Michael. 94 (n. 93)
Embree, A.T. 95-96 (n. 98)
Encyclopaedia Britannica 86 (n. 9), 86-7 (n. 10-12), 89 (n. 47-8)
Essays Relative to the Habit 90 (n. 60)

Farquhar, J.N. 94-95 (n. 94), 96 (n. 103)
Field, Harry M. 11, 93 (n. 89)
Frazer, R.W. 87-88 (n. 22), 89 (n.46)
Friend of India 7, 54, 105 (n. 267), 106 (n. 305)
Fuller, Mrs. Marcus B. 92 (n. 77), 93 (n. 85), 95 (n. 95)

Ganguli, Prabhat Chandra. 107 (n. 318)
Garratt, G.T. 85n. 1), 95-96 (n. 96)
Gopal, Ram. 92-93 (n. 82), 104 (n. 250-51)
G.B. Parliament 106 (n. 292, 299)
Griffiths, Sir Percival. 87 (n. 14), 93 (n. 83), 94 (n. 93), 97 (n. 117)

Heber, Reginald. 53, 59, 105-106 (n. 275, 293-8)
Hiriyanna, M. 107 (n. 323)
Indra 100-101 (n. 181-2, 184), 101-102 (n. 195, 197, 206), 103 (n. 216, 219)
Ingham, Kenneth. 106 (n. 300)

Jha, Mahamahopadhyaya Ganganath 89 (n. 52)
Johns, William. 88-89 (n. 29, 32-4, 50, 52), 100 (n. 170-3, 176-8)

Kane, P.V. xi, 34, 37, 97-98 (n. 118, 120-5, 128), 99-100 (n. 151-4, 156, 159, 193, 169), 100-101 (n. 181-2, 185-6, 190, 196, 198-203), 101-103 (n. 204-208, 210-211, 215), 103-4 (n. 223, 225-6, 228-9, 233, 235),

107 (n. 322), 108-109 (n. 336-8), 110-111 (n. 347, 350, 354), 112 (n. 360-1)
Karmarkar, D.P. 105 (n. 257)
Karve, Irawati. 86-87 (n. 10)
Kavanagh Boulger, D.E. de. 105 (n. 272, 277-8)

Lair, M.A. 107 (n. 316)
Lanman, Charles Rockwell. 35, 100 (n. 181), 102 (n. 209, 211)
Larson, Gerald James. 107 (n. 320)

Macdonnell, A.A. 35, 36,103 (n. 211-3)
Macmunn, Sir George. 96 (n. 104)
Mahadevan, T.M.P. 98 (n. 129-30), 101 (n. 192), 107 (n. 323, 330)
Mahfuz-ul-Haq, M. 92 (n. 81)
Maitra, Harendranath. 96 (n. 105), 98 (n. 140)
Majumdar, R.C. 87 (n. 14, 21), 87-88 (n. 17, 22, 35), 88 (n. 44), 89 (n. 51), 90-91 (n. 70-71), 91 (73-74), 94-95 (n. 94), 98 (n. 136), 99 (n. 143-44, 155), 100 (n. 179), 101 (n. 191), 104 (n. 245), 105 (n. 254-55, 258-60, 263), 107 (n. 317),
Marshall, P.J. 88 (n. 25-7), 90-91 (n. 70), 99 (n. 148)
Marshman, John Clark. xi, 50, 105 (n. 266), 106 (n. 291, 302-3, 306, 309)
Mayo, Katherine. 92 (n. 79), 93 (n. 87)
Mill, James. 89 (n. 52), 90-91 (n. 70) 92-93 (n. 82)
Missionary Register 61, 106 (n. 300)
Monier-Williams, Sir Monier. 85 (n. 3), 87 (n. 15), 91 (n. 72), 96 (n. 106), 109 (n. 339), 110 (n. 345)
Muir, Peter. 90 (n. 69)
Muir, Ramsey. 85 (n. 5)
Murty, K. Satchidananda. 101 (n.192)

Nandargikar, G.B. 97 (n. 113)
Nehru, Jawaharlal. 94 (n. 93)
New Standard Dictionary 85-86 (n. 8)

O'Malley, L.S. (ed.) 93 (n. 88), 107 (n. 320)

Pandey, B.N. 89 (n. 51), 95-96 (n. 98)
Panikkar, K.M. 86-87 (n. 10)
Parkes, Fanny 64, 106 (n. 310)
Parvate, T.V. 105 (n. 256)
Pegg, James. 61, 90 (n. 63), 106 (n. 304)
Penzer, N.M. 85-86 (n. 5, 6, 9), 87-88 (n. 12, 16-18, 22, 24), 96 (n. 108), 98 (n. 136), 103 (n. 222)
Philips, C.H. 96 (n. 107), 106 (n.311)
Pinkham, M.W. 87 (n. 11)
Powell-Price, J.C. 91 (n. 94)
Prasad, Ram Chandra. 99 (n. 145-7)
Raychaudhuri, H.C. 87 (n. 14, 21), 88 (n. 44), 90-91 (n. 70-1), 99 (n. 143-44), 100 (n. 179), 101 (n. 191)
Renou, Louis. 87 (n. 11)
Reincourt, Amaury de. 91 (n. 74), 95-96 (n. 98)
Roberts, P.E. 11, 88-89 (n. 36, 45), 90 (n. 61), 93 (n. 91)
Roy, Rammohun. 7, 64, 105 (n. 269-71, 276), 107-108 (n. 314, 319, 324-5, 327-9, 331-2)

Sambada Bhaskara 53, 105 (n. 273)
Sastri, P.P.S. 100 (n. 168)
Sastry, N. Yagnesvara. 93 (n. 89)
Sen, Surendra Nath. 91 (n. 74)
Sewell, Robert. 88 (n. 28)
Sharma, Arvind. 108 (n. 332)
Sharma, Neeta. 99 (n. 160)
Sharpe, Eric J. 73, 108 (n. 334)
Shay, Theodore L. 105 (n. 253)
Shore, Frederick John. 55, 105 (n. 279)
Singh, Iqbal. 105, (n. 261)
Singer, Milton. 107 (n. 326)
Singhal, D.P. 94 (n. 93)
Slack, D.B. 90 (n. 59), 106-07 (n. 313)
Sleeman, W.H. 64
Smith, George. 89 (n. 51)
Smith, Vincent A. 85-86 (n. 8), 90-91 (n. 70), 96 (n. 107)
Spear, Percival. x, 88-89 (n. 41-3, 49) 97 (n. 117), 104 (n. 236-7), 107 (n. 316)
Spiegelberg, H. 73, 108 (n. 333)
Spratt, P. 97 (n. 115)
Srinivas, M.N. Foreword, 86-87 (n.10)

Tahmankar, D.V. 104-105 (n. 248, 262, 264)
Tawney, C.H. 105 (n. 281)
Thomas, P. 100-101 (n. 181-2)
Thompson, Edward. x, 11-12, 20, 85-86 (n. 3, 7-9), 86-87 (n. 10), 87 (n. 19-20), 89-90 (n. 53, 55, 57, 61-2, 67-9), 92, (n. 79), 93 (n. 83-4, 88), 94-97 (n. 94, 97, 100-102, 106, 110, 116-7), 98-99 (n. 133, 141-2), 103 (n. 224)
Tinker, Hugh. 92 (n. 80)
Tylor, Edward B. 96 (n. 109, 111-2)

Upadhyaya, Bhagwat Saran. 36, 103 (n. 214)

van Buitenen, J.A.B. 100 (n. 167)
Vivekananda 92-93 (n. 82), 96 (n. 105)

Walker, Benjamin. 98 (n. 122), 98 (n. 132)
Walker, F. Deaville. 90 (n. 66)
Ward, William. 61, 85 (n. 2), 89 (n. 53), 106 (n. 301)
Webster's Dictionary 103 (n. 220)
Whitney, William Dwight. 103 (n. 217)
Wilkins, W.J. 86 (n. 9), 89 (n. 55), 98 (n. 85), 104 (n. 235), 107 (n. 319)
Williams, Raymond Brady. 98 (n. 133a)
Wolpert, Stanley A. 104 (n. 239, 248-50)
Woodruff, Philip. 85 (n. 7), 88 (n. 23), 92-93 (n. 78, 83), 95-96 (n. 96, 98), 103 (n. 227)
Woods, James Haughton. 111 (n. 353)

Young, Katherine. 109 (n. 343), 111-12 (n. 356)

Zaehner, R.C. 88 (n. 30)

SUBJECT INDEX

Abhimanyu 101-102 (n. 204)
Age of Consent Bill and Act 43, 46
Aja 97 (n. 113)
Akbar x, 20, 25, 27, 49, 94 (n. 93)
Albuquerque x, 3, 49, 87 (n. 22)
Amardas, Guru 49
Amherst, Lord 7
Aṅgiras 16, 29, 31, 101-102 (n. 195, 206)
Aparārka 16, 22, 29-30, 31-2, 34-5, 94-95 (n. 94), 102 (n. 211)
Āpastamba 32
Army 7
Arnold, Edwin 12, 20
Aurangzeb 5

Bai, Ahalyā 49, 94-95 (n. 94)
Bāṇa 15, 22, 40, 94-95 (n. 94)
Bandyopadhyay, Anandaprasad 53
Bangadoot 53
Baptist Missionary Society 6, 58
Basu, Ananda Chandra 44
Battle of Plassey 6, 87 (n. 14)
Battuta, Ibn 23
Bengal x-xi, 6, 7, 10, 27, 50, 59, 67, 92-93 (n. 82), 94 (n. 93), 108-109 (n. 337)
Bentinck, Lord William x, 7-8, 11, 17, 43-5, 49-50, 52-55, 63-4, 67, 85 (n. 5), 91 (n. 75), 93 (n. 90), 94-95 (n. 94), 96 (n. 107)
Bernier 27, 100 (n. 178)
Bhadrā 33
Bhattacarya, Gourisankara 53
Black Magic 16
Bombay 50
Bowrey, Thomas 4
British x, 6-7, 8, 12, 20, 22-23
British Government 45-48
British Governmental Interference 104-105 (n. 252)
British Legislation 11
British Policy of Non-Interference 94 (n. 93)
British Raj 9, 13, 47, 87 (n. 14), 89 (n. 55), 91-92 (n. 76), 95-96 (n. 98, 105, 107, 114)
British Territories 13
Buchanan, Rev. Claudius 58, 60
Burning of Heretics in Europe 94-95 (n. 94)
Buxton, Mr Fowell 61

Calcutta 10, 58-59
Carey, William 6, 8, 58, 63, 106 (n. 305)
Cārudatta 30
Charnock, Job 4
Chowdhury, Kalinath Roy 53
Christian attitudes 7, 19, 60, 89 (n. 51), 93-94 (n. 92), 96 (n. 105)
Concremation 1, 29-30, 39, 53, 98 (n. 128)
Conti, Nicolo 88 (n. 28)
Conversion of India 57-58, 64, 91 (n. 73)
Cornwallis, Lord 51
Court of Directors 7, 94 (n. 93)

Dadu 54
Daniyal, Prince 20
Deb, Radhakant 37, 63
Derozio 55
Devakī 33
Devaṇabhaṭṭa 16, 22, 94-95 (n. 94)
Disposal of the dead 35, 36
Droṇa 33
Dubois, Abbe Jean Antoine 57, 109-10 (n. 344)
Duḥśalā 15
Durant, Will 91-92 (n. 76)

East India Company 51, 55
Excommunication 53

Female principle 16-17
Fitch, Ralph 87 (n. 46)

Gallic Myths and Rites 13
Gāndhārī 33
Governor General 7-8, 44, 54-55, 63, 67
Greeks, 3, 5, 13, 19, 20-21, 23
Greek Myths and Rites 12
Greek sources 1
Graham, Maria 51, 64
Gujarat 17

Haimavatī 33
Hall, Fitzedward 35
Hamilton, Walter 51
Harding, Charles 85 (n. 7)

Hārita 29, 32
Haraṣavardhana 40
Hawkins, William 21
Heber, Reginald 59-60
Herbert, Thomas 4
Hindus xi, 21-22, 23-24, 39, 45-48, 49-51, 52-3, 55-6, 57, 61-5, 72, 74, 76, 82, 104-105 (n. 239, 248, 252)
Hindu reformers 8, 31
Holwell, John Zephaniah 90-91 (n. 70)
Hypergamy x

Imperialism 9
Improvement of Indian Morality 45
Indian Fear of Forced Conversion 45-6
Indian National Congress 47
Indian Scholars x
Indo-British Relations 12, 47
Indo-Western Encounter ix, 2, 4-5, 10, 13, 97 (n. 104)
Indumatī 97 (n. 113)

Jauhar, Jauhur, Javehur xi, 21, 85-86 (n. 10), 99 (n 151)
Jehangir 23, 49
Jāmbavatī 33
Jerome (St) 3
Judiciary 7

Kabir 54
Kaegi 100 (n. 181)
Kailāśa 40
Kālidāsa 97 (n. 113)
Kauravas 33
Keteus 2, 87 (n. 12)
Khusrau, Amir 21
Killing of women 108-109 (n. 337)
Kṛpī 33
Kuntī 26

Lord, Rev. Mr 5, 26-27

Macaulay, Lord 10, 51
Macdonald, K.S. 44
Madhva 30
Madirā 33
Madras 26, 92-93 (n. 82)
Mādrī 25, 33
Mahāśvetā 15
Marathas x, 49, 92-93 (n. 82), 94-95 (n. 93, 94), 96 (n. 107)
Marshman, John Clark 50
Marshman, Joshua 8, 60
Marx, Karl 93 (n. 90)
Medhātithi 16, 21, 94-95 (n. 94), 102 (n. 206)
Mill, James 90-91 (n. 70)
Missionaries ix, 6-7, 8-9, 31, 49, 52, 57, 59-62, 63
Mughals xi, 6, 27, 93-94 (n. 92)
Müller, Max 35, 100 (n. 181)
Mullick, Munshi Mathuranath 53
Muslims (Muhammadans) 19-20, 22-3, 46, 47, 91 (n. 73), 97 (n. 117)
Mutiny 8-9, 91 (n. 74)

Nanak 54
Nau'i, Muhammad Riza 20, 25
Nizamat Adalat 7, 55
Nobili ,de 4

Onesicritus 87 (n. 15)
Orthodox 8

Paiṭhīnasi 29
Pāṇḍu 25, 33
Parkes, Fanny 63-4
Pārvatī 86 (n. 9)
Phenomenology 73-4
Polo, Marco 3
Polygamy xi
Poona 92-93 (n. 82)
Portuguese 96 (n. 107)
Prabhākaravardhana 40
Pre-pubertal marriage xii
Privy Council 8, 10, 93 (n. 86)
Propertius 3
Pṛthā 15

Rajputs x, 12, 92-93 (n. 82)
Rajputana x
Rāmānanda 54
Rao, Peshwa Balaji 49
Rati 15, 40
Rāvaṇa 33
Reform of Hindu Society 49-50, 62
Religious Tolerance 45, 62, 91 (n. 73)
Remarriage 103 (n. 219), 109 (n. 339)
Rohiṇi 33
Roy, Jagmohan 93-94 (n. 92)
Roy, Rammohun x, 7, 9, 11, 17, 22, 43, 45-8, 51, 52-3, 60, 63, 67-9, 70-1, 91 (n. 75), 93-94 (n. 90-92), 95-96 (n. 98), 105 (n. 261)
Rukmiṇī 33

Śaibyā 33
Sairandhrī 33
Sarasvatī 40
Sati—see under "Suttee"
Satyabhāmā 33
Savantvadi 94-95 (n. 94)
Scythians 12
Serampore Trio 6-7, 60, 90 (n. 59)
Sexuality, Male Control of xiii, 56

Shikoh, Dara 92-93 (n. 82)
Shore, Frederick John 55
Siculus, Diodorus 87 (n. 12)
Sinha, Ramakrishna 53
Slaves 5, 33, 85 (n. 6)
Slobb, Sir Andrew 104 (n. 239)
Smith, Courtney 94-95 (n. 94)
Smith, Vincent 90-91 (n. 70)
Strabo 3
Suicide ix, 16, 34, 61, 73, 94-95 (n. 94), 102 (n. 206), 108 (n. 336)
Śukra 32
Superstitions 45
Supreme Goddess 17
Surat 26
Suttee/Sati: as an alternative to pilgrimage by dying man 81
— abolition of x, 1-4, 8, 13, 17, 29, 43-5, 47, 49-50, 51, 54, 57, 59, 63, 72, 87-88 (n. 22), 90-91 (n. 70), 93-94 (n. 92), 101 (n. 239)
— abolition of, causal factor in mutiny 91 (n. 74)
— absence of male performing 97 (n. 113)
— academic interest in 59
— actions of orthodox party after abolition of 105 (n. 256)
— admiration of 19-24, 33, 73, 96-7 (n. 105), 113
— application of term 1, 39, 85 (n.5), 103 (n. 220), 107, (n. 315), 109 (n. 342)
—approval of 98 (n. 128)
—argument for 99 (n. 151)
— as a barbarous rite 13, 108 (n. 335)
— as a Bodhisattva 112 (n. 359)
— as a duty 31, 36-37, 40, 50, 102 (n. 206)
— as a form of yoga 82-4
— as a grief reaction 30, 40
— as homicide 8, 29, 52, 58, 61, 74, 108 (n. 336)
— as an inferior act 50-1, 54, 68, 70, 94-95 (n. 94)
— as a marital custom 92-93 (n. 82)
— as a means of protecting widows 97 (n. 117)
— as a moral justification fo. British Rule 9, 91-92 (n. 76), 95-96 (n. 96), 97 (n. 114)
—as a rite or custom 85 (n. 5)
—assumed British approval of 94 (n. 93)
— auspicious nature of 74, 76, 80, 110-111 (n. 352)
— condemnation of 21-4, 29, 33, 94-95 (n. 94), 98 (n. 132), 99 (n. 151)
— confirmation of Indian sources of gruesome details 100 (n. 178)
— contrary to Vedas 94-95 (n. 94)
— in contrast with strictures against killing 58
— description of rite 2-3, 4, 21, 26-7, 40, 61, 76-7, 87-88 (n. 22)
— discrepancy in account of 101-102 (n. 204)
— dissuasion from 25, 27, 40, 93-94 (n. 92), 100 (n. 169, 108-109 (n. 337), 110 (n. 350)
— distribution in U.S. of tracts against 90 (n. 59)
— earliest records of 87 (n. 11)
— empathy for view of widows committing 96 (n. 103)
— falsification of Veda in support of 35, 100 (n. 181), 102-103 (n. 211, 215)
— first legal sanction of 102 (n. 206)
— following cremation of husband 39, 85 (n. 6), 104 (n. 235), 110 (n. 351)
— Freudian interpretation of 97 (n. 115)
— goal of 31-2, 69, 72, 80-2, 84, 87-88 (n. 22), 112-113 (n. 360, 361, 362, 363)
— Hindu apologetic attitude towards 97 (n. 114)
— Hindu assistance in abolition of 54
— Hindu criticism of 54, 97 (n.117)
— Hindu indifference to arguments concerning 54
— Hindu minimization of British role in abolition of 93 (n. 90)
— Hindu opinion of 8-9, 41, 53, 55, 59-60, 73-4, 94-95 (n. 94), 97 (n. 117)
— Hindu reaction to Western sensationalisation of 92-93 (n. 82)
— Hindu response to 49, 58
— impact on community of women withdrawing from 110 (n. 349)
— inauspiciousness of too many 110-111 (n. 352)
— incidence of ix-x, 7, 27, 30, 50, 59-61, 89 (n. 46, 50, 53), 92 (n. 79), 94-95 (n. 92, 93), 101-102 (n. 204)
— Indian attitudes, etc. etc. see under "Hindu"

— indifference of onlookers to 54, 64
— involuntary 5, 21, 26-7, 84, 88 (n. 28), 93-94 (n. 92)
— justification of 55-6, 90-91 (n. 70), 99 (n. 151), 102 (n. 205)
— last legal 87 (n. 14)
— monopolisation of credit for abolition of 11
— native attitudes, etc.—see under "Hindu"
— not considered a widow 112 (n. 357)
— not viewed by Hindus as homicide or suicide 108 (n. 336)
— opposition to 15, 17, 101 (n. 192)
— opposition to abolition of 45, 50, 60, 94-95 (n. 94)
— origin of 12-13, 56
—"original" 104 (n. 235)
— penances for women withdrawing from 110 (n. 350)
— persuasion to perform 25, 83-4, 108 (n. 336)
— press campaigner against 53
— prevention from 53
— prior to husband's death 40-1, 104 (n. 235)
— public opinion in Britain 57
— reaction to 2-5, 6-7, 8-9, 10, 13, 16, 19, 22-3, 58, 61, 73-4, 87-88 (n. 22)
— refusal of wives to commit 85 (n. 5)
— religious dimension of 58, 73, 81-2, 101 (n. 193), 103 (n. 215)
— restrictions in performance of 30, 32, 110 (n. 350)
— sensationalisation of 10, 92-93 (n. 82)
— symbolic 34-8
— testing resolve of woman to perform 110 (n. 349)
— trivialisation of 92-93 (n. 82)
— Vedic allusion to 38, 97 (n. 113), 103 (n. 215)
— voluntary 26, 54, 65, 96-97 (n. 10), 108-109 (n. 337)
Swaminarayan, Shree 17

Tagore, Dwarkanath 53
Tagore, Prasanna Kumar 53
Tali 109-110 (n. 344)
Tanjore 92-93 (n. 82), 94-95 (n. 94)
Tavernier 27, 100 (n. 178)
Thomas, John 6
Thompson, Edward 10-12, 20
Tilak, Bal Gangadhar 43, 46-8, 105 (n. 256)

Udney, George 59
Uttarā 15, 101-102 (n. 204)

Vasudeva 33
Vedavatī 33
Vedic approval of widow remarriage 103 (n. 219)
Vedic opposition to rites 52
Vellore Mutiny 54, 63
Vidyālaṅkāra, Mṛtyuñjaya 50-1, 63
Virāṭa 16, 21, 94-95 (n. 94)

Ward, William 8, 61
Wellesley, Lord 59
Western womanhood x
Widows ix-xiii, 1, 10-11, 16, 23, 29-30, 32-3, 35-7, 41, 49-52, 56, 69, 74-6, 78, 79, 80, 84, 88 (n. 29), 101 (n.193), 103 (n. 215, 220), 109 (n. 342), 111-112 (n. 335, 357, 360, 363)
Widow burning xi, 7, 13, 33, 36-7, 44, 49, 52, 61, 94-95 (n. 94)
— widow's goal 78-80
— widow's inauspiciousness 74, 80-1
— widow's life 75-6
—widow as an ogress 75, 80, 109 (n. 342)
— widow's religious dilemma 81-3
— widow's rites 109-110 (n. 344)
— widow sacrifice 12
— widow as a yogi 79, 82
Widower xiii
Wife/wives 2-3, 17, 23, 34, 89 (n. 46)
Wilberforce, William 60
Wilson, Horace 45, 85 (n. 5)
Withington, Nicholas 21
Woman/Women 17, 74, 77, 89 (n.52)
Woman's responsibility for husband's death 78
Woman's role 77-8

Yaśomatī 40, 104 (n. 235)

Zamindar 58